Where Have You Gone Mickey Mantle?
is published by GK Creations.
This book is available at special quantity discounts
for fund-raising or educational use.
Please address all inquiries to
GK Creations, 5 WhiteCliff Dr., Pittsford, N.Y. 14534.

ISBN 0-9652026-0-7

First Printing 1996

Library of Congress Catalog Card Number 96-94331

Cover illustration - Jim Williams

Acknowledgments

I want to thank all the wonderful friends I have made in my life. Many are in the following pages; those who are not are in my "book of life."

A very special thank-you is owed to Maurine Johnson, my sister, for her encouragement and many hours she donated, editing a large portion of this book. Maurine is a teacher in the Webster, New York School District. She teaches English as a Second Language and is fully dedicated to her students. Maurine has been a guiding light for me, during all my years.

Ralph Hyman who is a professional sports writer and sports editor, has helped me immensely with this book. Ralph is a perfect gentleman and truly a great friend.

Jim Williams has also helped me a great deal. He has donated his tremendous knowledge of publishing, design and precious time to this book. The front cover was designed by Jim. Thank-you.

Where Have You Gone Mickey Mantle?

To Jill, Adam, Lauren and the love of baseball.

In memory of Mickey

In memory of Marilyn and Bernard Kravetz

Preface

The story of Mickey Mantle has often been told from the perspective of his magnificent career and all his heroics. This book takes a closer look at Mickey's role in the evolution of baseball and his striking impact on the salary structure and economics of the game, along with the physical and emotional levels of play. Since the retirement of Mickey Mantle, there has been a withering of the great American pastime.

The purpose of this book is to simply recapture those beautiful moments of truth, when baseball was the American pastime. Mickey Mantle represented the last breed of a **true superstar**. What has evolved from that point is watered-down stock. Now, there is a whole generation of real baseball fans, who were in love with Mickey and with sandlot baseball, in more innocent and uncomplicated times when they were growing up. We all wanted to "be" Mickey. Some admitted this openly, but most of us had this dream in our hearts and only now talk about it.

Growing up with baseball as the focal point of our lives made for an extremely happy childhood for millions of baby boomers. Throughout this book I recall some of those beautiful and euphoric days. We now long for the good old days. Our children just don't understand the way it was, just as most of us do not truly understand their computer generation. Where have you gone Mickey Mantle?

Forward

My son Adam was born on Joe DiMaggio's sixty-fifth birthday. As a sixteen-year-old, Adam already has a keen eye for sports talent. He is a darn good athlete and a computer whiz kid. He is a great kid. Both Adam and my daughter Lauren have an extremely close relationship with Jill and me.

Lauren, at fourteen, **lives** to play softball. Even though she is a straight "A" student, there still are occasional "bad" days in school. Once she gets on the softball field, she tells me that everything is then perfect. What an arm and, boy, can she hit! She is also a great daughter.

My dear wife Jill is the most tolerant person in the world. She is the <u>perfect</u> grammar school teacher, wife and mother. I know that she is not enamored with baseball. I think she has heard a few baseball stories around our home. She is the greatest.

PREFACE
FORWARD
CONTENTS
INTRODUCTION
CHAPTERS:

Introduction

America is absolutely a great place to live and raise a family. We have freedom of choice. We may have more leisure time than most others and are ridiculously better off than our parents' generation, although that cycle is about to be broken for a majority of our children.

What bothers me is when I ride by a baseball field on a sunny afternoon, after the *Little League* season ends, and there is absolutely nobody there! Have we lost our appreciation for our American pastime or do we just have too many choices? Will our children study hard to learn, or study hard to earn an "A" and forget the material? Does anyone really enjoy practice for the sake of practice and learning past a perfunctory or socially acceptable level? If a few kids are playing ball on that field, it is truly an anomaly.

As I look around, I will notice a few joggers, some children who are rollerblading, some playing soccer, Frisbee, Frisbee football, roller-skating, roller-skiing and I guess that some are home playing Nintendo or searching the Web. Others are taking trips of major proportions, in gymnastics, floor hockey, ice hockey, ice skating, early football camp, shooting hoops, swimming outdoors and indoors, bumping the volleyball, practicing their musical instruments, rehearsing OM, at play practice or even doing oodles of homework. These are all very commendable and important activities in a child's development. The problem is obviously that we tend to make our children "Jacks of all trades and masters of none." If we encourage them to master a hobby or activity, we must realize the price of our time commitment.

Their peer competition seems to be ferocious and sometimes discouraging.

What is the solution to this "affluent choice" society? I guess that parental involvement and guidance will help to ensure quality learning and fair play in these activities. That is the reason that I, like **so** many other dedicated parents, spend endless hours running *Little League* and other competitive organized sports programs. It may knock my friends' socks off to find out that I am not particularly fond of *Little League* type programs. I have dedicated myself, with a tremendous amount of vigor and deep involvement over the past ten years or so, for the sole purpose of making it as good as it possible can be, <u>for our children.</u> Many other parents agree that is the only game in town, so we should try to make it fair and fun during competition. The beauty of growing up in the fifties and early sixties was that there was a better game that was played on the sandlots, if you could find a field!

This book is meant to be a stress reducer. While the material may be revealing and add some facts and chronology to your baseball memory bank, it is now time to wander off into the delight of your childhood. Enjoy!

10

CHAPTER 1

<u>A Perfect Start</u>

It was a weekend in late September and I was just five and one-half years old. The 1954 World Series was on in our house. We now had our first television. It was a black-and-white Magnavox console. The picture was usually clear after it warmed up. The New York Giants were playing the Cleveland Indians. My memory of what happened then is still vivid.

My father Bernie was watching the game for a while and relaxing, although I was undoubtedly disturbing him by running around "like a wild Indian". He was too kind to complain about my distraction, but he was also a master psychologist in parenting. He invited me to watch the game with him and I really wasn't that interested. He then coaxed me by offering me a spot to lie down on the couch, right in front of where he was lying. As I was only five he could easily see the whole screen around me without any obstruction. He seemed anxious to settle me down. I now know that the game was tied. As I comfortably cuddled into my father, he achieved his goal. I was finally watching and he could concentrate on the game.

Soon Vic Wertz was up to bat (who was already 3 for 3). He rocketed the first pitch to the deepest part of the Polo Grounds. Willie Mays made *the catch* and the phenomenal throw to complete a double play. My father literally jumped off the couch and promptly said, "Bobby, don't you *ever* forget that catch because they will call that the best catch ever made, in history." The tone of his voice was so serious and so demanding that I almost thought that I had done something very wrong! Often, throughout my life he would quiz me as to who hit *the* ball. Once out of dozens. . .and dozens. . .and dozens of quizzes I became quite frustrated with his insistence, I jammed my channels, choked and mumbled Vic Power! Oh boy, was he pissed!

Obviously, my father had a tremendously keen eye for sports and truth. He didn't converse all that much, but was so intelligent when he did, that you had better listen. He was a most remarkable person to all who knew him. My sister Maurine is just like him.

This episode is my first clear recollection of depositing of a special event of baseball, into my memory bank. Basically that play and interpretation of it became my frame of reference for all defensive play and a level of greatness in sports. This happening had an enormously positive psychological impact on me, at a most critical stage. I dare say that I have seen Dave Winfield make a more phenomenal catch as a Yankee, leaping into the left-field stands, but the circumstance was not as critical. I also thought that Ed Kranepool's catch in the 1969 Series was as good or better. I really was also elated watching Joe Rudi's gem in the sun, and Lou Piniella's "blind" one-hop stab of the ball and decoy, to hold Rick Burleson's advance to just one base, in the "greatest play-off game" ever. Although Lou didn't actually catch it, he still "saved" the game and ultimately another Yankee World Series victory! Mays admittedly did make even better catches in his remarkable career. I cannot ever remember actually seeing a better throw than Willie's.

I truly believe that this day was meant to be.

Thank you Dad, you were *the* GREATEST!

CHAPTER 2

A Happy Childhood on the Sandlots

The term "superstar" has been changed almost as many times as there are sportscasters or writers. When was the word coined and how was it applied? The use of the word became prevalent in the 1960's and clearly proliferated with TV and selling a game to the public as had never been done before. If we remember back to the fifties, we saw DiMaggio leave and only then (because of longevity), were there Mays, Mantle and Koufax who could potentially fill this void. Reflect back on the stars who were not included in this elite category. Roberto Clemente, a younger Henry Aaron, Don Drysdale, Duke Snider, Campy, Al Kaline, Frank Robinson, Ernie Banks, Warren Spahn, Eddie Mathews, Yogi Berra, Whitey Ford,

Harmon Killebrew, Ken Boyer, Curt Flood and Bob Gibson (with an ERA of 1.12!) come to mind. Another group, yet to come were Pete Rose, Reggie Jackson, Johnny Bench, Willie Stargell, Ferguson Jenkins, Ron Santo, Billy Williams, Jim Palmer, Rod Carew, George Brett, Mike Schmidt, Yaz, Joe Morgan, Tom Seaver, Nolan Ryan, Brooks Robinson, Catfish Hunter and the great Thurman Munson. But clearly these tremendous players were not heralded in the elite M-M-K class. So why Mantle, Mays and Koufax? To understand why, first we have to reflect back on the attitudes of the times.

The fifties and early sixties were a real neat time to grow up. I use the word neat because it served us well back then. Choices were more neat and tidy like "eat what is on your plate for dinner, or eat nothing at all." The United States of America was very patriotic and united as one country, after coming together to win the "War to End all Wars." Our GIs had recently returned home proud, and started a whole booming generation of baseball bambinos. Our hero and leader was General Eisenhower, who by the way, was very good luck for Mickey when he attended games. We also were in the process of saying good-bye to our celebrated hero Joe DiMaggio.

As a nation, we were hungry to prosper and enjoyed our national pastime on weekends. Most families had very few material goods. We lived in small homes that were in close proximity to each other. Small neighborhoods were conducive for pick-up baseball games day and night. We were lucky if we had a brand new ball and a few decent bats. If the ball ripped open, we would put another piece of electrical tape on it. A new ball cost 39-50 cents, far too much for our limited budgets. If the bat

15

cracked a little, we artfully pounded a tiny nail into it and then taped over it. My friend Andy Grassi was exceptionally adept at that. We could not easily afford a real good bat which might cost up to $5.00.

Most families purchased their first black-and-white televisions and the "Game of the Week" often featured the great New York Yankees. Often I tell my recollection of my first glimpse of TV in 1953, and children look at me as if I have come from a different and far-off planet. Surely their children will give them the same look of amazement, with similar stories about before they had computers.

For the record, my first show viewed was *"The Howdy Doody Show"*, at a neighbor's apartment. Soon it was baseball on Saturday afternoons. Vivid joyful memories filled out childhood, of yet another improbable late-inning comeback with Yogi taking one low and outside, and still driving it into the corner for another win. We learned with Mickey and Yogi and the gang, that it "was not over, until it was over!"

Television soon picked up the dramatics and calculated which game would have the probability of the largest market draw, which coincided with the relatively new blossoming business of advertising.

The great New York Yankees symbolized baseball and all its heroics. It was a clear-cut easy sell to the public. The networks were enchanted with the amount of advertising revenues that could be generated by a solid audience. The public was glued to the excitement of the Yankees, whether they loved them or hated them. There seemed to be nobody neutral. The Yankees in the fifties and sixties were to TV what Arnold Palmer, with his great Ipana smile, and golf were to TV in the sixties.

The average person was poor but did not even realize it. We never worried about our next meal because our parents worked hard, but toys were a real luxury. That in itself, strengthened our moral character.

Baseball games took a very serious role in developing one's manly reputation. From the second we arrived at the field, we had to be ready for "war," including a possible fist fight for the exclusive use of the field. We really never had more that one of those baseball fights where nobody threw a punch. But just the possibility of somebody encroaching on your turf made it a serious event. Tempers would have often flare while agreeing or disagreeing on the ground rules. Even the selection of teams was an artful and special process. The embarrassment of being selected late would loom large, and often reflected your place within your peer group.

Each field had its own rules which were traditionally understood. Typically we started when there were enough players to make a good game. Someone would yell, "Let's choose up." Rarely was a single player larger than the game and able to delay this process. Then came the artful game of "throwing the bat" to gain first selection of players available.

The object of this paramount exercise was to be the one who could "cap" the bat on the last turn by putting his hand over the entire knob of the bat, and also have all of his fingers touching the opponent's hand at his last position.

The challenge started by a simple toss of the bat to your opponent's representative. He would catch it at a point which he thought was advantageous to his hand and/or forearm size and experience. At that starting point, the two players would work their way up the barrel with a scissors cut, full-hand play, or try to cap for a win. This also included a **legal** move of putting your elbow flush on your opponent and running your forearm flat up the bat and going for the successful crowning.

The representative to compete in this exercise already carried a special leadership role on your team. The fate of your team's fighting ability was portrayed in how this person carried himself even if he lost. The representative would not necessarily be the team captain, although he was most often a decent ball player and a good judge of talent. The real captain would often be selected first as the best ballplayer. The representative would be the equal of a co-captain or second in charge, which still carried some weight. Other important criteria for representatives might be:

1) You had the only or best bat, or ball.
2) You were the biggest kid and posed a potential physical threat.
3) Your father owned the field that you were about to play on.

My friends Jim Williams and Wayne Howe were intimidating. Jimmy at times came in to warm up and hummed the ball from the mound, over the backstop. (Once, two pitches in a row!) I'm sure that Jimmy wanted to "be" Ryne Duren! Wayne was full grown at thirteen and as strong as any man I knew! He often carried a rumble chain in his pocket. Wayne was also a good friend like Jimmy, and protected me for years from potential physical abuse.

Some fields didn't waste the time of "shooting the bat" but preferred "shooting fingers" (no, not Jack McDowell and Ted Williams style) but "once, twice, thrice. . .SHOOT." Often the arguments would commence

18

here when captains disagreed who had "odds" or "evens," or was it one time or the best of three shots? The better players were always cognizant of wasting a lot of time at the beginning of a game because inevitably the game would run into dinner or darkness and invariably at a crucial time of the game.

We had to fight our own battles on the ball field without the protection of the *Little League* organizations for the vast majority of games. Even as a young man, or an exceptional "Tomboy", we inherently understood that *Little League* was a small show for the parents, but 8 a.m. to 5 p.m. was when you learned and developed your skills and character. If someone called you an SOB you handled it yourself. You could always tell a person's character in clutch situations.

Playing sandlot ball gave us a beautiful opportunity to develop and fine-tune our skills. I distinctly remember taking every pitch for two days straight, at Hosea Rogers School, and learning how to hit to right-field. Those seventy swings served me well for the next thirty years when the occasion called for it. Most *Little Leaguers* don't get seventy bats in two seasons and the parents want them to be as good as Mickey! We also never rated people by materialistic goods or by race, creed or religion. Yes, the fifties were a more pure and beautiful world.

One of the biggest thrills was when Andy and I got to talk "live" to Johnny Blanchard. We met Blanchard in 1962 in a department store, Sibley's. This monumental meeting occurred twenty to thirty years before card shows. Current shows have opened up continuous access to big name stars. In 1962, this was an extremely rare and unique opportunity. That was a great day.

Andy and I asked Johnny Blanchard how we could

make it to the big leagues. He quickly responded that there was no substitute for practice. Practice is precisely what we did all day long which equated with eternal happiness. Even if there was no official game you could usually find two others to play "500", "Home Run Ball", "Whiffle Ball", APBA" Baseball, or as a last resort, hours of "Chinese Baseball"" off the front step, forever simulating the ultimate clutch play to win the game with two outs in the bottom of the ninth!

Homerun ball was like a modified version of the TV show *Homerun Derby*. Each player had to hit the ball into the neighbor's yard or over some bushes to score runs and keep his at-bats. The neat thing about it was that your alias for game's sake, would be one of your idols, not your own.

My lifelong friend Mark Hurwitz always wanted to "be" Hank Aaron whereas his older brother Garry, also still my friend, wanted to "be" Enos Slaughter, which were wise choices for the times. Garry was almost two years older and had remarkable power even at a young age. The only problem was that he broke the same basement window in my house, SEVEN times! My father was great. He didn't get real mad until about the fourth or fifth time. Besides, parents of that generation didn't ever use the "F" bomber in their vocabulary because that would not be raising their children right. I dare say, we heard a *few* "hells" and "damns". Most importantly was that I always wanted to "be" Mickey Mantle.

Baseball is what we lived for day and night. If a rainy day prevented us from playing, we would "fly" or "flip" baseball cards. That was an art in itself. First of all, we would need to know the inherent worth of a player and his card. There certainly weren't any price guides in the fifties and sixties that we knew about. Next came each person's artful ability to convince your opponent that your card was of equal value to his, although you really believed that yours was not as valuable as his. You needed knowledge to add credence to your case. Thank God that we weren't flying against a renegade like Bill Veeck or Charlie Finley. Often a friend would have to mediate this affair.

Then came the art of flying towards the designated wall where the closest pitch won both cards, with special rules for "leaners". The astute flyer would use an iron fist to give a flatness and an advantage in flight. Often, if the corners were bent or the card was bowed, air resistance could embarrassingly abort the flight before that all important tenth foot.

Sometimes bad feelings were had, and mothers would have to intervene in order to save friendships. But, all in all, it was a great way to be entertained in the world of baseball. A loss would not necessarily be devastating because nobody with any sense would gamble with their Yankees or other favorite players.

We also occasionally clothespinned our "scrubs" to our bicycle spokes, although this didn't set well with me, as being sacrilegious. If someone happened to lose a few cards it would give him the rational excuse to buy yet again another pack of cards for a nickel. Hold your breath because Mickey might be in there. The euphoria of finding a Mantle card was equal to that of seeing Mickey hit that homer off Sal Maglie, and Yogi jumping into Don Larsen's arms. That was a better October 8th!

There were no western teams until the very late fifties (1958, thank you, Mr. O'Malley and Mr. Stoneham). Great rivalries had already emerged between the Yankees and the Boston Red Sox, and, of course, the Yankees and the Brooklyn Bums. Communication of sports events was far from perfected. There were no instant replays, color commentators, and statisticians for each game situation.

Often during the action, Old Dizzy would lose control from when the moment the ball was hit to the moment when he "slud in there pardner"! Local newspapers sometimes did not even publish complete boxscores or the schedules of upcoming games, let alone starting pitchers. How did we survive without ESPN?

The transistor radio was a most cherished possession that could link us into the dream of baseball and the very rare agonizing of a Yankee defeat in the World Series, which included The Gloomiest Day. Certainly not every kid had his own transistor because they ran about five dollars. A paper route served hard-working kids well. They could save up for a decent transistor, and it also taught discipline and character.

Andy and I had the same route but mine was in the morning and his in the evening. My other best friend Roger Goebel also had a paper route, and was a naturally talented athlete who could play every position well with little practice! Roger bought a nice transistor radio with his paper-route earnings. He advised me of which model and where to make this important purchase. There was even a knack to get those darn radios to work continuously, especially during a late-inning Yankee rally. We appreciated heroes but they had to be *true* heroes and not "fly-by-nights".

Our parents' teaching credo was "if you are going to do something, then do it right" (or not at all). There were no short-term superstars by definition.

CHAPTER 3

<u>The Perfect Uncle</u>

Raymond Kravetz was my father's "kid" brother and just eleven years and some months older than I was. Not only was he the big brother that I never had, but he was the kindest man you could ever imagine.

How kind is kind? Well, once, when Ray was a child and had wanted a bicycle for many years, my grandparents finally "scraped up enough" money to make the big purchase. At last, after waiting and waiting, the big day arrived and Ray got his brand new bike! Immediately, he took it out for a little spin. A little while later Ray returned ... without his bike or any bike!

"Raymond, where is your bike? Are you hurt? Did you have an accident? Are you okay? Where is your bike?"

"No, Mom," said Ray, "I met a little kid that **loved** my bike and would never have a new bike because they are poor. So I gave him mine."

Uncle Ray would have given anyone the shirt off his back to make them happy.

In early May, 1958, my family was struck with tragedy when my mother passed away at a young age. I was nine; my sister Maurine was all of twelve. My father never let us feel sorry for ourselves. Our family would just stick together and hang tough. Ray was always around to help whenever we needed him.

During that first week of May, we had a house full of people. After a few evenings, Ray said to me, "Let's go out for a little while." We hopped in his car and went to Wallack's Drug Store. Ray knew that I was already Yankee and Mickey crazy. He bought me two full uncut sheets of 1958 Topps baseball cards and a whole mess of packs! When we were at the cash register, I decided that baseball was going to be my fulfillment for life. I was in deep thought. I reiterated that promise to myself until it was perfectly clear and imbedded in my head! I smiled at Uncle Ray and we went back to the house. At home I opened the packs and out popped a brand spanking new 1958 Mickey Mantle!

Ray certainly didn't quit there. He was a perfect uncle for years to come. Whatever it was, Ray was constantly giving to the situation. He was in the stands when Mickey hit the game-winning homer off Barney Schultz in the 1964 World Series. The ball landed fairly close to his seat. When he got home, he was a little mad because he wanted to catch the ball and give it to me! Uncle Ray will be in my heart forever.

24

CHAPTER 4

The Perfect Job

At twelve, I took the third job of my life. I had been cutting lawns and shoveling driveways since I was nine. I was lucky to get the morning paper route. I had to tell a little white lie about my age, because I was supposed to be thirteen, to be eligible. This splendid opportunity netted me between six and seven dollars a week!

The cash earned was a great benefit, but not the best one. The year was 1961. I had already been "ripping open" the paper and immersing myself in the box scores since the end of 1956, Mickey's Triple Crown season. I scrutinized every box score, every day (for about thirty years). The only problem was that my father ordered the evening paper only. That was much too late in the day to quench my thirst. Baseball results via radio were not dependable, and did not give the real statistics. My father didn't have the time to read the paper each morning before work and probably couldn't afford both issues.

I struggled through the horrendous winter of 1961 in upstate New York. At times, I had doubts about my sanity. Making your own tracks at 5:30 a.m., with wind chills far below zero and in the dark was tough. My father, who was a tough WWII GI, advised me to hang in there. The paper route experience taught me strict discipline, mental and physical toughness and the value of money.

Soon, the beautiful spring of 1961 started and the Yankees were looking good. Mickey had hit 40 homers and Roger 39 the previous season. I was a bit miffed that Roger had nipped Mickey for the 1960 MVP by a few points. But I was glad that Roger was a Yankee. I started getting up at 5:00 a.m. every day without an alarm clock. Each morning, I became deeply engrossed in the box scores by 5:05, after skillfully maneuvering the paper out of the middle of the wired bundle. Rarely did I rip one. I then sat on the rest of the paper bundle and read. 5:30 came much too quickly, because I had to go to work delivering, and not yet had my fill of baseball data. Even school now seemed to be more tolerable, with this great start to each day.

It was arguable the **best** summer in baseball history. Mickey and Roger were on "the chase". Need I say more? If that wasn't enough, I soon ran into a large financial increase.

Norm Hurwitz, who is Mark's father, asked me what time I received my paper delivery on the weekday mornings. I responded that typically I got them between 4:15 and 4:45. Norm was a very hard-working man. His family owned a coal business. He left every single morning for work at 5 o'clock sharp. He said that if I could get his paper to him by 5 a.m. and not one second later, that he would tip me one dollar each week! That was an instant raise of about 15%. I reset my head for 4:30 and was then reading the box scores by 4:40. I would finish this exercise of euphoria during breakfast.

That's when I got the notion of saving articles about Mickey and Roger. Norm's house was directly behind my father's. I missed his delivery only twice in the next year and one-half. Once the papers arrived at 5:10 or so. The other time I missed him by 30 seconds. I still swear that my Timex was correct.

Norm was six foot, left-handed, and a superb athlete. He was exceptionally good at ping pong, pool, bowling, golf, fishing and baseball. He had a million great stories about the great old ballplayers including the "Gas House Gang". Rochester was the farm club of the St. Louis Cardinals for many years.

Norm always wanted to "be" Stan the Man. He was also very cool. He drove a mint 1959 pink Cadillac, with those enormous fins, and always told us great jokes.

His wife Annice was always dear to me. My mother passed away when I was nine. Norm and Annice were always extremely supportive. Mark and I played together as kids nearly every day for ten years. Thank you, Norman and Annice. Happy 75th birthday, Norm.

Andy had the evening paper route that covered the same geography as my paper route. I'm not sure when we met, but soon we were collecting from our customers together, every Friday night. Andy was Yankee nuts like me. Mickey was God. Soon we were playing in each other's sandlot games and later teamed up to play organized hardball and competitive softball games.

Years later, I was honored to be Andy's best man at his wedding. Upon waiting for our cue to proceed to the altar, Andy looked really nervous. He was always poised in the last inning of a game and could always hit in the clutch. But then, Andy looked as if he was going to pass out. He really had nothing to worry about because Joan was a doll.

To break the tension, I quickly started telling Andy about how Yogi would often eat sliced banana and mustard sandwiches in the dugout, for a snack. We were roaring with laughter. The clergymen gave us a bit of a dirty look when we hurried in a few seconds late! **Andy's ceremony was** in the morning. I guess we were late early.

1961 was the ultimate.

CHAPTER 5

Mickey and the True Superstars

Factors that defined the word "superstar" are numerous. First and foremost was longevity of being the best at your trade. Joe DiMaggio was a superstar and fully embraced by the public, but the great Ted Williams was not quite up to his standard! The problem with Ted was that he wasn't "doing it right". Obviously it was an image thing. Can you imagine winning the triple crown twice (1942, 1947) and neither year being selected by the sports writers as the league MVP! Today a player would call his lawyer.

Also unthinkable was the notion that players would ever play for more than one team in their careers. Each name would be synonymous with the Yankees, Giants, or Dodgers. Only Willie Mays ended his career with another team and just a little too late.

One can argue that TV was in its infancy and Henry Aaron was as good as the elite but lacked exposure. The other side of the coin is that "Home Run King" Hank was not of *awesome* power and never topped the 50 mark (47, 1971). Also, Aaron started a few years after Mantle and Mays. Later in his career his superstar status could not be denied. How many men have hit the magical 50? Twelve to be exact, as Albert Belle just accomplished this heroic feat, and how many did it twice? Babe did it an amazing four times, Ralph Kiner and Jimmy Foxx did it twice and so did Mickey and Willie. Sorry, Hank, so "close but no cigar" as we used to say in the fifties!

Sandy Koufax was *the* best at his trade and far outdistanced the rest of the field. Some call him the greatest of all time or at least the greatest lefty and also naming Walter Johnson as the best righty. Between 1963-1966 Koufax averaged 24.25 wins a season, an amazing 298 innings pitched per season, 37.5 starts, 22.25 complete games and an ERA of a measly 1.86. He pitched no-hitters in four straight seasons, the last one being a perfect game. Opponents hit a mere lifetime .205 against him, which is the second best mark in history. Nolan Ryan is at .204. Koufax signed on in 1955 for a bonus of about $14,000! Granted that Sandy did not have longevity, due to his forced retirement because of his arthritic condition. Let's leave the statistics behind, because statistics and words could not do justice in accurately describing his ability to rise to the occasion and win in the toughest situations. You had to see him perform to understand how great he was. The circumstance for Koufax was quite often having lack of run support.

Nobody in the history of baseball has had a lower earned-run average in post season play! The one expression that was true was that "the only thing that was tougher than Koufax, was Koufax after a loss", or may I add, when all the marbles were on the table. Hall of Famer Willie Stargell was always quoted as saying that "hitting of Koufax was about as easy as eating soup with a fork." The only possible equal was someone who would "guarantee" to strike out the first nine, pitch at least 100 no hitters and win 2,500 games in his career, and could throw a two-humped blooper!

Willie Mays was born in 1931, the same year as Mickey. They both came up to the majors in 1951. Jackie Robinson had paved the way for Willie. At the Polo Grounds Mays ruled in the outfield. He could outrun almost any ball that was hit. If you don't believe me, just ask Vic Wertz. He would dive, slide, spear and leap to catch any fly ball hit. His nonchalant patented basket catch proved that he was most often in the right spot before the ball actually got there. His first home run came off the great Warren Spahn and the ball *left the yard,* at the Polo Grounds. Nothing much changed for nearly the next twenty years.

Today a middle infielder may hit .246, drive in 51 runs on Astroturf, which equates to the art of shooting marbles with a bat on concrete, go to arbitration and win 1.7 million dollars for the next year! It's obvious that longevity is no longer a factor. In 1951 Mickey was signed by Tom Greenwade, for a $1,150 bonus and $140 a month until the end of the year. Now we all know that times are different but come on, we now have the average salary of nearly one million dollars per year and nearly two million for the Yankees! That is five to ten times more than the president makes and they are not **all** having better years than he!

Mantle had to keep proving himself year after year. That was clearly the mind set of the fifties. Koufax's great domination came a little later but he was truly awesome. I am not belittling Greg Maddux but Koufax was a level above. The public required everyday players to keep up their performance levels for at least ten years, but more convincingly fifteen years. This exact sentiment was expressed to me by my father's Uncle Sam who lived in Brooklyn during this era. Living in New York and being a respected elder and an astute baseball fan, (although he rooted for Brooklyn) qualified him to be somewhat of an expert. I'm sure there were experts in every family! In many a discussion, it was always **"Well. . .we'll see if he can keep this up?"** My answer was always, "Just watch."

To illustrate this sentiment, let's look at Mantle's record. Reflecting back, I wonder how Mickey felt. In 1955 he won the home run crown with 37 and had a slugging percentage of .611. That made him a superstar, right? Wrong. So in 1956 he won the Triple Crown, *and* runs scored, *and* the slugging percentage with .705 and now he was *eligible* to become a superstar! Then his name was on the national ballot and he was under the microscope, for intense scrutiny. Wanting to earn superstar status, he returned to hit a mere .365 and his boss wanted to decrease his salary for having a downslide in performance! Yankee GM George Weiss tried to cut his salary by $5,000, because Mickey didn't again win the Triple Crown!

The brass of the Yankees, as well as other owners, often negotiated in a ruthless manner. Recently, author

David Halberstam related the bitter feelings that Vic Raschi carried with him for the rest of his life, after being traded to the Cardinals in February of 1954, by GM George Weiss.

After the 1956 season when Mickey won the Triple Crown, he wanted a raise that would double his salary and bring him up to $65,000. Weiss threatened him with a detective's report that would hurt his image and Weiss did not have to add "to say nothing of your marriage." Statements of that nature were not published in the 1950s as they are today. To our generation, Mickey was pure, innocent, and our hero and role model, for the good of the game!

The press supported the hard-nosed negotiating of the team owners. When Joe DiMaggio had his first big season in 1937 (46HRs, 167 RBI,.346 AVE., SA. 673) he wanted $40,000 for 1938. The press got on his case for not accepting $25,000. Yankee owner, Jacob Ruppert, said that $25,000 would make him "financially independent for the rest of his life." DiMaggio was then fighting the owner, with no recourse other than to give up baseball, the press, and his public image.

In 1933 the great Jimmy Foxx won the Triple Crown and owner Connie Mack wanted to reduce his salary from $16,670 to $12,000. Foxx had hit **only** forty-eight homers, down from fifty-eight! In 1934 Gehrig had one of his fabulous years (49 HRs, 165 RBI,.363 BA.,.708 SA, 210 Hits). He had to battle to stay at $23,000!

It probably wasn't until the comeback in the 1958 series against the Braves, or with the home run title of 1960 and the arrival of Roger Maris, that Mickey's status became "etched in stone." On August 14, 1960, Mickey failed to run out a ground ball and Casey immediately replaced him with Bob Cerv. That was the last time in his career that he did not act like a superstar. He redeemed himself that same season by winning another home run title, another pennant and having a fantastic World Series. A superstar had to perform up the highest standard of greatness for quite an extended period. This took ten to fifteen years of great playing. That's longevity with superstar results.

How good was a superstar in the true sense of skill? Mickey, Willie and Sandy were clearly superior to the rest of the field in all aspects of the game. Looking at the elements of America's pastime, we first recognize hitting, fielding, throwing, and running. Add to this list power, clutch, winning and psyche.

The raw hitting potential of Mays and Mantle was awesome. Mickey could instill fear into the opposing pitcher and fielders with every at bat. He had raw power and was virtually a .300 hitter, his whole career. (.298 to be exactly only because of his extremely debilitated knees in the last two seasons). Mickey had a neck and torso coil and uncoil like nobody else, pound for pound. Those massive arms extended through the ball with a vicious impact. Along with hitting the ball a player must be able to run. The fact of the matter is that when Mickey was growing up in Oklahoma, he was able to run after jackrabbits and catch them! Yes, you can look that one up!

From the left-hand side of the plate he was timed at 3.1 seconds going down to first. That was the fastest of anyone ever timed. He also has been timed as the fastest runner around all four bases. Mickey had 6 inside-the-park home runs in his mighty career. It wasn't until late in his career that he ever got beat in a spring training foot race, by a much younger Vada Pinson.

Can you imagine "playing in" for a bunt on Mantle with his awesome power? No way! No one would gamble his life and body parts so foolishly.

Opponents played very deep and prayed that the ball wouldn't maim them for life. How could Mantle possibly be thrown out on a bunt? He was recognized as the best two-strike bunter in the game. "He was the greatest two-strike bunter the game has ever known," said Arnold Hano in Sport Magazine in 1965. Yes, the lost art of bunting was still considered an integral part of the game for a complete player. I wonder if Jose Canseco has ever attempted one? It would be interesting to ask the 1995 Seattle Mariners if they would trade Joey Cora for Jose Canseco.

Mickey also had a tremendous eye at the plate. He walked often and in 1957 had an on-base percentage of .515 which was the ninth best in history. His lifetime on base percentage was .423. Mickey also owns the record of games played for the Yankees with 2,401, so he used this magnificent talent often, and continuously won at a remarkably high percentage, twelve pennants and seven World Series in a span of fourteen years!

Running has more dimensions than just raw speed and going from home to first. Mantle, with Aaron and Mays, were also the best base runners of their time. They could go from first to third with impeccable judgment. Mantle also slid so hard that he would have fielders so concentrated on him barreling down on them that they often would miss the ball. Then there was that classic pop-up slide, where Mickey was always ready to advance to the next base. Nobody instilled fear in the fielder like Mickey, when he was breaking up a double play because of his unique combination of speed and power. If you ever saw

Mickey's hook slide, it was also unforgettable.

A fielder would envision the impending doom of getting clobbered by a ninety-mile an hour freight train and tend to give the slightest bit so that he was not standing directly in his pathway, but just close enough to make the tag. Down would come Mickey right at him like a ton of bricks, and at the last split second would slide on the outside of the other side of the bag and hook his foot in, SAFE! There was no defense other than call the ambulance or a mortician first. There had been a few who tried foolishly to hang in there and hold their ground but often they would end up sprawled on the outfield grass!

For the record, Mickey's stolen base percentage of successful attempts was .801! In Mickey's first twelve seasons, he stole at a successful clip of .816. In 1959 he led the league in base stealing proficiency by stealing 21 out of 24 attempts. Mickey also led the Yankees in steals 8 different times. In 1961 he hit into only 2 double plays! After Canseco made a big deal of being the first 40/40 man, homers and stolen bases in a season, Mickey simply commented that, "If I wanted or needed to, I could have done that easily a few times, or 50/50 if I knew that it was such a big deal!" So much for the unknowing and the unsophisticated critics of what Mickey *couldn't* do because of his legs.

Speed is a wonderful thing. Just ask Don Larsen, who watched Mickey outrun a Gil Hodges line drive in left center and spear it across his body, to save his perfect game. (Also thank Andy Carey and Gil McDougald for their great infield play.) Speed is such a great commodity that it has literally made a career.

Herb Washington was a "designated runner", with world class speed, for Charlie Finley. He played on the

1974 World Champion Oakland A's, as a terrific designated base stealer. He owned the indoor world record in both the fifty and sixty yard dash. He is also a very nice person and now resides in Pittsford, NY.

Maybe if Mickey wasn't so fast, he would have missed stepping on that drain pipe in the 1951 World Series. Then his accomplishments would have been Ruthian! It's just amazing that Mays hit that ball. It really is a small world of fate.

Mickey could catch anything in sight, which took so much pressure off Hank Bauer, who was not a fleet-footed outfielder. Mickey won the gold glove in 1962, led the league in assists in 1954 (20), in fielding in 1955, 1959, and 1966 in 97 games in the outfield (1.000) This exceptional talent also make for a winning team, which is not measurable in the statistical analysis of the game, which seems to be so relied upon today. Managers would have to recognize talent and manage it to their best benefit. For instance, when Mickey was covering his territory (from left center to right-center) Casey or Ralph Houk were afforded the luxury of putting another slugger in the outfield. Often this was Yogi, Elston or Johnny Blanchard.

Now once you catch the ball, what are you going to do with it? Well, the truth of the matter is that they never talked about Kaline's or Colavito's arms until Mickey retired. Often Mickey played down his fielding abilities in post-career interviews. I'm not quite sure of the reason for that. My guess was that it was just the shy, boyish, mild-mannered demeanor that he always carried. That modest posture was also evident after slamming a home run and putting his head down to not embarrass the pitcher. You never saw Mickey wave his arms or give animated gestures. It's still a home run, just like when Larry Bird would steal a pass and lay it in for two points. Is it worth more to showboat and make a stupendous dunk? It may be worth less if you infuriate your opponent.

Mickey's strong and accurate arm was the end result of the raw speed, grace, the energy of the legs and the granite-like muscular body, followed by the ball's flight. The astute baseball fan realizes that Willie's throw was even better than "the catch." Very few runners would even think of going on Mickey, which typically kept the double play in order, and the Yankees that much closer to coming back to win another!

The first time that Casey saw Mickey was in the spring of 1951 when Mickey was just nineteen years old. According to Robert Creamer in *"STENGEL: His Life and Times,"* "Mickey had such speed that he caught balls that other outfielders couldn't get near." After Casey put him in center-field he noticed that his arm was impressive. Upon throwing out a runner at the plate, Tommy Henrich, who had been around and knew the level of play commented, "That was the best throw that I have ever seen!" It was Henrich and Joe D who taught Mickey how to play the outfield. Casey commented "My God, the boy runs faster than Cobb".

The great Bill Dickey was arguably one of the best catchers that ever lived. He was as great as Johnny Bench defensively, (I am not taking anything away from Bench's great RBI production) and he was as tenacious as Munson in the clutch, batting .300 in ten of eleven years and driving in over 91 runs on average. (This fact is remarkable since he hit after DiMaggio and company and there weren't many people left to drive in.) Dickey was as agile as Bench and physically as rugged as Rose diving into Fosse. If you don't believe me just ask Carl Reynolds. One game against the Washington Senators, Dickey was frustrated because of not throwing Reynolds out at third base and Reynolds kept running and slid into and decked Dickey, who retaliated by breaking Reynolds' jaw with one punch at home plate.

Dickey played in the era of Ruth, Gehrig and DiMaggio and understood all about Yankee Pride. He was the magical mentor who turned Yogi into one of the best fielding catchers. They knew Yogi would be a great hitter. Dickey was also instrumental in teaching Elston Howard.

When Dickey saw Mantle he commented that "he's going to be the greatest player ever." The first article in the local newspaper *(The Democrat and Chronicle)* had Casey calling Mickey a "clouting fool". Soon Casey changed his title to "the Phenom."

As a matter of interest, with no one on base, Mickey always threw a knuckleball back into the infield, and a tremendous one at that. Only Gil Hodges, as a non pitcher, was said to have a better one. This potentially saved the wear and tear on his arm for years. I wonder if Mickey could have pitched, like the Babe?

Paul Richards is generally credited with being one of the smartest men in the history of baseball. He spent his life in baseball and managed the White Sox and Baltimore when Mickey was in his prime. With only eight teams in the league, the visibility of the players was enhanced to the point of really seeing the opponent quite often and realizing his true abilities over the long haul. Richards commented about Mickey, **"He can hit better than anyone else, he can field better than anyone else,**

he can throw better than anyone else and he can run better. What else is there?"

Casey had his own point system which equated a point for each run "earned or saved" per game. If you were Ozzie Smith and saved two runs a game by remarkable plays in the field, you would be rated worthy of two points. Mickey was worth five points a game and his closest competitor Al Kaline, about two and one-half to three. As Al Kaline was signing autographs one fan commented, "You are not half as good as Mickey Mantle." Al did not take offense but simply agreed with that astute young fan and commented "Son, *nobody* is half as good as Mickey Mantle."

One key factor about Mickey was that he was a switch hitter with brute strength from the right side and phenomenal flight from the left side. Remember, when Mickey played at Yankee Stadium, the base of the bleacher wall was 461 feet in left-center. Over the wall was almost guaranteed to be 500 feet. Mickey hit more balls into the bleachers than anyone else. Tony Kubek, who has a very accurate recall of events, often spoke of the years when Mickey hit, for sure, 30-40 that would have been out of any other park, in one season when he hit forty plus anyway. His first righty, gargantuan shot was on April 17, 1953, in old Griffith Stadium in Washington. This 565-footer ticked the side of the scoreboard, flew out of the park and landed across the street. Red Patterson, the Yankees press agent, found a tape measure and "voila", the ERA of the "tape measure" began. Thank you, Chuck Stobbs.

On Memorial Day, 1956 Mickey connected with a fastball and the ball started out for the moon. The ball struck near the top of the facade, high above the third deck in right field. No ball to date has ever left Yankee Stadium. Oh, by the way, the wind was blowing in a bit! The Rochester *Democrat and Chronicle* called Mickey, "the boy with the golden bat." That day, Mickey hit two homers that the newspaper called preposterous! The first was blasted off Pedro Ramos. That beauty was witnessed by Frank Crosetti and Dickey. Crosetti and Dickey played with Ruth and Gehrig. They both agreed that they had never seen a ball hit farther! In the second game, Mickey launched one into the right-field bleachers, a feat done by few others.

The beauty of baseball is that it is paradoxical, much like life itself. The foul line is fair and the team on offense does not have the ball. Most of the time things do not seem to change all that much which is a good day for the statistical analyzers! Other days one can be amazed at some of the heroic feats, like Bobo Holloman pitching a no-hitter in his first start or Bucky Dent's homer!

On that Memorial Day, nothing much changed. Mickey hit two enormous home runs and went 4-8 in a double header, the Yankees winning both ends.

In the International League the Miami Marlins' starting pitcher, Seth Morehead, was hit in the hand by a line drive, and had to leave the game. Satchel Paige came in to pitch and finished the game, allowing no hits! His "two-humped bloopor" must have been hopping.

Mickey had been on one of his power binges at the time. Just a week earlier he had hit a home run in Kansas City, that cleared two fences, went over a forty-foot embankment, and traveled out of the park. Perhaps that ball was drafting the *Sputnick!* That was just a regular day. During that same game, Billy Martin charged off the bench to go after relief pitcher Tommy LaSorda. Of

41

course, that fight was broken up without a punch being thrown.

Left-handed, all he did was hit two off the facade in Yankee stadium. The second off Bill Fischer traveled nearly 400 feet at the point of contact and 119 feet high, was still rising, as declared by the radio announcer, and hit with a great thud! Can you imagine if the facade had been back one more foot and the ball cleared and then bounced freely on concrete. Even on a bell-shaped curve of physical force, this arguably would have gone 800-1000 feet Or maybe it would have topped Foxx's homer that hopped a train in Boston and ended up in Chicago, or Josh Gibson's that landed in "Pitchburgh" the next day but was caught. Paul Richards may have said it best declaring, "Mantle hits the most splendid home runs since Ruth. The ball jumps off the bat with great velocity and distance."

Some critics may question the combination of hitting home runs with longevity. The fact of the matter is that Mickey came up the same year as Willie and going into 1965, when Mantle was nearly incapable of playing due to his injuries, he still led Willie in career home runs by one "round-tripper" with about 500 less at bats! As Ol' Casey used to say, "If you don't believe me you can look it up!"

CHAPTER 6

The Rochester Red Wings

Growing up in Rochester, N.Y. was great. Although there was no major league team around (the Yankees were 400 miles away) we did have exciting, quality, AAA professional baseball. Also, I lived just a few miles away from the ballpark.

"The International Association, founded in 1877 is frequently described as the first minor league." The Rochester Red Wings were members of the National Association beginning 1902. The International League started in 1912 and the Red Wings became a charter member of the league. From 1927-1960 the Red Wings were affiliated with the St. Louis Cardinals. From 1961 to present the Red Wings have been affiliated with the

Baltimore Orioles.

The era with the Cardinals was before baseball expansion and a time when players didn't move up until they were "seasoned". Great players performed here in a beautifully designed ball park, then called Red Wing Stadium. In 1968 the name was changed to Silver Stadium after the late Morrie Silver. Mr. Silver was instrumental in raising sufficient funds, through selling stock to the public, to keep the Red Wings in Rochester.

Stan Musial, Pepper Martin, Marty Marion, Red Schoendienst, Specs Toporcer, Erv Dusak, Russ Derry, Estel Crabtree, Bob Gibson, Jack 'the Preacher' Faszholz, Don Richmond, Harry 'the Hat' Walker, Marshall Bridges, Timmy McCarver (at 17 years old!), Joe Cunningham, Joe Altobelli, Bob Kuzava (who was Casey's man in the clutch against the Dodgers in the Series two years in a row!) Bob 'no-hitter' Keegan, Gene Green, Gene Oliver, Ruben Amaro (who could throw you out from deep short better than Shawon Dunston) and the legendary Luke Easter played here during the Cardinal years. In 1932, Red Wing, George Puccinelli led all of the minor leagues, with an average of .391 (400 or more AB).

After the St. Louis association ended and Baltimore started, we had the pleasure of watching Bobby Grich (who was acclaimed minor league player of the year two consecutive years), Don Baylor, Leon Wagner, Pete Ward, Andy Etchebarren, Steve Bilko, Boog Powell (32 home runs), Davey Johnson, Doug DeCinces, Tom Phoebus, Darold Knowles, Mike Epstein, Merv Rettenmund, Roger Freed, Curt Blefary (31 home runs), Mark Bellanger, and Cal Ripken!

As youngsters we lived and died with the Red Wings.

Quite often they had a very good team. It was always a thrill to go to the park. There were no bad seats, excitement was high and the grass was real. One day Andy Grassi stopped over to see my sister! He had an application for a contest to become the Red Wings' bat boy. For all intent and purposes, Maurine wrote the essay and Andy won second place in stiff competition! It's a good thing that Maurine was often the official scorer of our Little League teams. Often the opponents parent scorekeepers would have to reconcile their score book, and walk over to see hers. Second place resulted in Andy being assigned as the bat boy for the Visitors. He became friendly with Jake Gibbs of the Yankees (Columbus) and many more major leaguers to be.

Some other visitors who played here were Yogi Berra, Roger Maris, Willie Stargell, Rocky Nelson, Duke Carmel, John Roseboro, George "Sparky" Anderson and Don Mattingly.

Some of the most astonishing moments happened when the Red Wings played the Havana Cubans. A *very* light-hitting Red Wing named Ron Kabbes started those years at shortstop, and played both ends of one particular Sunday doubleheader. Frankly, I'm not sure if I wouldn't rather have Sandy Koufax at bat, who was as bad at hitting as he was great at pitching! Ron Kabbes always seemed to always be up with the game on the line and....WHIFF!

This happened as often as having the weakest kid in Little League, who was on your team of course, up to bat, in *the* clutch situation, and you would start praying. You're too good of a guy to ever pinch hit, because you wouldn't want to take this heroic opportunity away from the child to succeed, just once. Maybe, by a miracle the pitch would be a little wild and hit the bat, and go fair for a game winning hit! I'm still waiting for that play to happen in my lifetime!

Anyway, now you can more clearly understand the feeling when Kabbes was at bat. I'm not sure if Kabbes had ever hit a homer before! That day he proceeded to "be" Mickey! He hit a three-run home in the first game, followed by a grand slam in the second game!!! Cousin Stuie and I were totally astonished!!! Once when playing in Havana, Frank Verdi, who was a long-time popular Red Wing, got shot in the batting helmet, with a bullet!

The most exciting game was played at Red Wing Stadium on September 11, 1961! (As if that magical season needed any more drama!) A one-game playoff was necessary, against the Toronto Maple Leafs, to decide who was going to proceed to post season play. Mark and I wouldn't miss this one for the world! The Red Wings' "ace" and 15-game winner, Herb Moford, was going for the home team. I was confident of winning from the beginning. After seven pitches we were behind 4-0! Toronto then scored three more runs in the second, 7-0!

Jim Finigan, who was a light-hitting infielder batting .224, with just two homers and fourteen RBI for the season, came up to the plate. He then knocked in a run in the fourth, and the Red Wings were then down 8-3 going into the bottom of the seventh. Finigan filed out to lead off, but the Red Wings now had finally put on their hitting shoes, and began to go crazy! Finigan got up again in the same inning and drove in the go-a-head run 9-8!!!

By the bottom of the ninth, with the whole season on the line, the Wings were down again, 11-9! With one out in the bottom of the ninth, and one on, Finigan proceeded to crack one into the left-field bullpen and WE WENT NUTS! The ninth inning ended tied.

In the tenth inning the Maple Leafs failed to score. Soon the Red Wings had a rally going and I then kept telling Mark that Finigan was going to get up. Sure enough, Finigan did get up, with two outs and the bases loaded. I can still see his right-handed swing. It was as if he served the pitch, just as you slice a tennis ball, clean into right field, not too short and not too far! Mighty Jim got four hits and drove in six runs, and the Red Wings went to post-season play. I never heard that noise level topped, even when Luke put one on the moon. I told you that I felt confident from the beginning!

One of the most embarrassing moments of my life was due to eating peanuts and playing "the shell game". One evening, Garry, Mark, Norman and I were at the game and eating peanuts. For some reason I was not sitting right next to Mark, but one seat away from him, with Garry in the middle. Mark and I were both bothered by this arrangement. The three of us were having a great time carefully and silently placing our empty peanut shells on a man's hat, which he was wearing, right in front of Garry. Soon, with every added sneak placement, we were nearing the hats' capacity and our chance of getting caught We were roaring with delight with each new victory.

After a few innings Mark and I were openly discussing going down to the concession stands to buy something to eat. Garry loudly interrupted and said, **"Why don't you get some more peanuts?"** We were in stitches. We had had our fill, and so did the man's hat! At the concession stand Mark and I decided that we would sit next to each other, regardless whether Garry liked the new seating arrangement, or not. We wouldn't take no for an answer.

Upon returning, we announced that we had a new seating arrangement. Soon everyone switched seats, so I was now going in first and actually moved up three seats. I backed down the row with my head down, watching that I didn't spill any soda that was in my left hand. I then spun around and was beginning to look up and saw a fresh bag of peanuts in my vision! Immediately, I FLICKED the bag of peanuts with my right hand, *MUCH* harder than we would flick each other's ears and emphatically questioned, **"ARE YOU KIDDING?!!"** When I looked up I then noticed that Garry was no longer sitting next to me, with his new bag of peanuts, but a complete stranger was!!! I wasn't too embarrassed. At least Mark, Garry and Norman had the laugh of their lives. Of course, they have easily let me forget this moment over the years.

We learned a lot at Red Wing games, and a few years later I wanted to impart some of this privied knowledge to my brother-in-law, Howard Stoler. I only extend this privilege to special people that I can trust, and we truly are close, like brothers. Howard is about five years younger than I, but as smart as a whip. In his teens, we began going to Red Wing games, and he caught right on to the "shell game", which he is now teaching my son Adam at Oriole games!

Sometimes in our younger days, with our bladders bursting, it was hard to focus on the hat in front of us and also keep a steady hand! Once, we actually stayed for seven innings of a game. I must say that Max and Adele Stoler were the world's greatest in-laws , because

48

they just let us grow out of this stage. Unfortunately Max is no longer with us, except always in our hearts. Adele has been relieved of her responsibilities. They have been taken over by Howard's lovely wife, Donna Stearns. What an incredibly understanding woman she is!

It was a most memorable day in 1958 when Catfish Eggert and I saw the great Satchel Paige pitch. He *admitted* to being fifty-two at the time. He took the mound for the Miami Marlins and easily won the game, pitching brilliantly!

The most memorable shot that I ever can remember (out of hundreds and hundreds, if not thousands of games) was seeing Luke Easter hit a ball over the light tower in right-field. (We weren't old enough to see Estel Crabtree's in 1939). This was a majestic, mammoth moon-shot, that left me **yelling at the top of my lungs,** to Mark and Roger, over the wildly and noisy crowd, **"that went OVER the light tower!, that went OVER the light tower!!"**

Luscious Luke Easter was born on August 4 (Mark's birthday), 1915, in St. Louis, Missouri. He played for the Cleveland Indians from 1949-1953 and just briefly in 1954. I guess you can say he was just an unlucky guy, because he just missed being on the great Cleveland teams of 1948 and 1954! He also died tragically by a bullet, not intended for him, several years ago in Cleveland, Ohio.

But the International League was lucky to have Luke's services for a number of years with both the Red Wings and the Buffalo Bisons being the benefactors of his mammoth home runs and so many clutch RBI. He did hit 93 home runs for the Indians. In his prime years, he hit

49

nearly 30 per year, for three years in a row. The number thirty in a year was the benchmark of a "real" slugger. Some players are real good until it comes to the clutch and then choke. Other winners like Luke, step up their game.

Statistically, Graig Nettles was a very good home run hitter with 353 dingers for his career. The truth of the matter was that he was a great home run hitter because so many of his homers were hit in key situations when behind in the score or with the score tied late in the game! Easter's long doubles (they had to be) and home runs often came in the clutch and were majestic by nature. Maybe the longest ball that he ever hit was the time when we saw him lumber into third with a stand-up triple! That hit, off the scoreboard, was something. He could really turn on a crowd and his team.

Often Luke would donate his time to children and ride in Little League parades and make various appearances out of the goodness of his heart. The community loved Luscious Luke and his "Ruthian" or Josh "Gibson-like" homers.

My dear friend George Reiber grew up wanting to "be" Luke Easter. I met George and soon after he drafted my son Adam into the "Majors" of Little League. He also drafted me as the coach. I helped George as he was the manager. It was on the Little League field that George would often talk about Luke Easter. When George turned 40, I attended a small get-together, at his law office for lunch. I remembered that a relative had an old film of a Little League opening day parade, with Luke riding in a convertible waving to the crowd. I had a self-contained VCR from work and surprised George by showing him this brief clip of Big Luke five times. I don't think George remembered to eat a thing!

One day our softball team was on the field almost ready to start an important league game. The only problem was that we had just eight players and needed nine players to start. George was walking by because he was there picking up his son Corey from soccer. He mentioned that if we were stuck, that he would fill in, although he was worried about getting home late. He went to tell Corey and rushed back just before the deadline. George was wearing loose-fitting, old lawn-cutting sneakers, the kind that we all have been saving for the past fifteen years! I remind you that the level of that softball league is still competitive. We "stuck" George at first base because he is left-handed and filled his name in last in the order. He also hadn't played in years because of a recurring knee problem.

As usual, our team was down after the first inning. George got up in the second inning with two outs and drove in our first two runs with a solid base hit to right. Then with bases loaded for the other team and two outs, George speared a short-hopper in the hole between first and second, and beat the runner to the bag by one-half of a step!

In the top of the fourth we were still down and George was up, again with two outs, and again drove in two more runs, with a "seeing eye" but clean base hit between first and second!

In the top of the seventh inning we were still down by two runs and started to rally. "Wild Bill Brand", with whom I played for twenty-five years, got a clutch hit, followed by clutch hits by my dear doctor friends, Joe Kurnath, Rich Gagnier and Paul DiMarco. Coincidentally, all four of these teammates grew up wanting to

51

"be" Mickey! Just two days ago Jill and I had the pleasure of going to a party at the Kurnath's. Rich and Paul
were both there. Soon Paul came over to me and proceeded to tell me that he just went ballistic because his
"good" neighbor said that "Mickey wasn't that good!"
He had to vent his feelings and had no idea that I was
writing this manuscript. After nearly thirty minutes of
discussion about how we felt about Mickey, and without
tipping my hand, Paul then ended the conversation by
boasting that "if you wanted just one person up to bat in
the ninth, it would **always** be Mickey!"

That night, on the softball field, we didn't have Mickey
in our last inning, but we did have George, who then got
up and smashed a line drive to right, and drove in another run!

Now we had a lead for the first time in the game, 9-6,
going into the bottom of the last inning. The only problem is that, the name of our team is *Murphy's Law*. Sure
enough we started to come apart at the seams by drop-
ping two routine fly balls! With two outs and the tying
run at third and the winning run at second, the batter hit
another fly ball. I screamed at the top of my lungs from
the pitcher's mound "SQUEEZE IT!!" Scotty Lamarche
squeezed that fifth out and we won 9-8!

George went 3 for 3, with five RBI, and a sparkling
play, (saving two more runs), in "sandals", worrying
about getting home, with a bad knee, after not playing
for nearly ten years! That night he was Luke Easter!

In 1997 the Rochester Red Wings will be playing at
Frontier Field, a new stadium. The community has been
invited to support the team by purchasing a brick with
your name on it, to be placed in the "Walk of Fame".
George has purchased a brick and has requested that his

brick be next to Luke Easter's! For the record, I'm not particular about where they place the Kravetz brick ... but I'm sure that I would sleep better at night if it was not next to Ron Kabbes.

CHAPTER 7

APBA BASEBALL

About the time I was fourteen and fifteen, the ball field started separating the men from the boys. Pony and Babe Ruth League were great. The ball was coming in faster and going out farther. It was a great time because baseball still consumed our thoughts. We were still too young to drive and too shy to ask a girl out. Andy, Garry, Catfish and I were still playing and growing with each play. Other friends still had a keen interest even if they were not playing. Baseball still ruled and so did the Yankees. Life was still perfect!

Roger was busy playing a game called *APBA BASE-BALL*. (From the APBA Game Co. Inc., Lancaster, Pa.) It was a board game that was based on each team having a separate card for each player on the roster. Players' cards all listed every possible shake of two mini dice. They even supplied you with a nifty yellow shaker. Next to each combination such as 1-1 or 1-2 there was another number that translated into a strike out, ground out, double play, single, double, triple, home run etc. Almost every possible game situation was simulated. The better players had better translation numbers. The game also had a sliding scale for the skill of the pitcher that you were facing. 3-3 with a man on, might be a double against an "A" pitcher but would be a home run off a "B", "C", or "D" pitcher. The ratings were not bad but far from perfect. Very few pitchers were "A ballers"! One set of cards had Sanford "Sandy" Koufax as a "B baller", that was the same rating as the Braves Denny Lemaster, and the Senators Claude "Wimpy" Osteen!!! At least Warren "Hooks" Spahn was an "A baller", but Whitey Ford was not! The game was played with three outs and nine innings. I was invited to watch and was intrigued enough with the strategies and the competitiveness of the league that Roger was participating in. There was no room for extra participants and also the *COMMISSIONER*, Larry DePalma already had rights to the Yankees. Smart kid! I then purchased an APBA game.

Larry Tatelman was a Dodger nut and always had his team. Jerry Sharfstein always took the next best team available, the Giants. Murray Migdall switched from one mediocre team to another, but more often than not took the Twins. As you might imagine, the Yankees supplied me with hours of delight and always a first-place finish or a home run title. It was uncanny how many times 6-6, a home run, would show up on the dice for Mickey, Roger, and Yogi. The vast majority were even

55

legitimate!

All was not lost for Murray just because he was easily and often, the first team to get eliminated, from our pennant races. He could reflect on his talent, or lack there of, and make up some very unique names which kept the game loose and often in stitches. Pitcher Lee Strange became Lee Brown Strange because his pitching stunk. Murray was remarkable and a generation ahead of his time. I wonder if Chris Berman got stuck with the lowly Twins in his league? Although I can repeat very few of the names, I assure you that Murray was highly thoughtful and very creative.

Around a plethora of fights, even about how we could load the dice, shake the dice, how far off the ground the shaker had to be, where the dice landed and everything else imaginable, a good time was had by all, except Murray. *Shake, Rattle, and Roll* (and pray for a 6-6 when Mickey was up) were the sign of the times.

Last year when I was in Los Angeles, I gave Larry his Dodger deck! I also looked for the Twins deck but they weren't there. Murray probably took them and burned them one by one! I guess we won't be starting another league soon. Larry and I do though have a standing bet. Each year it's his Dodgers vs. my Yankees, (the real major league teams), year end winning percentage rules. This year I nipped him (as usual), by one game. How can you route for 'dem Bums'? Happy New Year, Larry.

CHAPTER 8

WHIFFLE BALL
Early Sixties

Whiffle Ball was a large part of our lives in the early sixties. Larry Tatelman, Paul Eggert, Murray Migdall and I spent hours "throwing our arms out!" This was serious stuff because we were gaining adult strength and knowledge, and firing that damn thing with all our might, from 12-15 feet! There are two distinctly different types of balls. The first is probably the true "Whiffle" ball. This is the type that had a series of elongated holes in one-half of the ball. The second is the plastic ball with no holes, but very pronounced raised seams.

Paul "Catfish" Eggert is probably the only player that

I played more innings with than Garry, Andy or Roger. He was the best pitcher in Little League majors by eleven, and started to dominate by twelve. Paul came from a rich tradition of the American pastime. His uncle, Elmer Albert "Mose" Eggert made it to the big leagues with Boston. Although it was only for "a cup of coffee," his name is in *the* book *(The Baseball Encyclopedia, The Complete And Official Record Of Major League Baseball)*. Paul's dad was Clarence Otto Eggert ... "Lefty" for so many that knew him. Don't let the name throw you. Lefty was 62 years or so, when I met him, at 10 years old. He was probably better than his brother on the diamond and knew virtually everything there was to know about baseball, because of his long past tradition.

For Paul's confirmation party, a number of his friends went on a picnic in a park. We all had our gloves and there was an expansive ball field adjacent to the picnic area. Lefty was 65 years old at the time. He started hitting fly balls out of his hand that were sending us so far back, that we needed the infielder to play rover, as the cut-off man, in order to get the ball back in. At this age I was now catching on a ninety-foot diamond, and could tell you within inches the distance of 127 feet, 4 inches. That is the distance of the "peg" down to second base.

Towards the end of this splendid sunny and perfect day of extended practice, Murray and I were *deep* out in right. Apparently Mr. Eggert was now warmed up because the balls were soaring over our heads. I promptly told Murray that the balls were traveling about three hundred and fifty feet! Murray and I moved way back. Now, every time that Murray caught or retrieved a ball, he threw it over to me, to make the long throw in. (Murray was a very "slightly built" shortstop, who now often runs marathons).

Everyone else except our cut-off man, and Paul who was catching for his Dad, had "petered out" of this hour-long or so, exercise. I was having a great time. Mr. Eggert announced "just a few more." All of a sudden the ball went flying over our heads by sixty feet or so! I yelled to Murray "oh my God". This one, I tell Murray, is 400 feet! Now I could not get the ball all the way back in. I had just attempted my throw when a ball goes *sailing* over my head! "Murray, look at *that* one!" "Okay boys that's enough, come in" yells Mr. Eggert. I quickly tell Murray to mark the exact spot where the ball was hit in the air, not where it rolled to. We knew within inches of the spot where the ball hit, identifying the bent grass. I ordered Murray to put his mitt there and leave it for a minute, because he retrieved that one. Murray looks a bit confused so I explained that we were going to go back to homeplate and walk this one off! We trotted in and I showed Murray precisely where 127 feet would be and from that spot another 127 feet would be, until we got to *the* spot. **Ol' Lefty just "cranked" one 427 feet!**

I probably set foot in the Eggert's house at least 300-400 times in my life. There was <u>never </u>a time during the baseball season, when Mr. Eggert did not have the Rochester Red Wings on the radio and he listened to each pitch. If a game was on TV, the television would be on, and the Red Wings would often be on in the background. Over the years, Mr. Eggert educated me about Rube Waddell, Rube Marquard's 19 straight victories with the 1912 Giants, Lefty Grove, George "Specs" Toporcer, Estel Crabtree (two of the greatest Rochester Red Wings), Luke Appling, Bob Feller, Walter Johnson's 56 consecutive scoreless inning streak, "Three Fingers Brown,"

"Chief" Bender, Pepper Martin, Red Ruffing from Boston and New York, Cy Young with 511 victories, Grover Alexander's 16 shutouts in a season, Rogers Hornsby's .424 average in 1924 with the Cards, Carl Hubbell's famous 1934 All-Star game, Al Simmons, Tris Speaker, Frankie Frisch, the "Fordham Flash;" "Big" and "Little Poison" (Paul and Lloyd Waner), Honus Wagner, Ty Cobb, Babe Ruth, Ted Williams, Joe and Dom DiMaggio and a host of other magnificent ball players. He was all smiles when he spoke of Tony "Push 'Em Up" Lazzeri, Lou Gehrig and Babe. He seemed often to talk of pitchers and most certainly influenced Paul's career.

Ruth played twice at Genesee Valley Park in Rochester. Mr. Eggert saw both games, including his mammoth home run. Rube Marquard pitched a brilliant game on the same diamond. Lefty also had witnessed that one. Marquard had a no-hitter going late in the game. He delivered a pitch and the batter didn't get real good wood. The ball was hit somewhat like a "Texas Leaguer," but hung up there a little longer and a bit deeper. His left-fielder let the ball land in front of him! Marquard then does a "beeline" to the outfielder and **"POP"**. One punch and Marquard "coldcocked" the guy, who is now out!

Mrs. Helen Eggert is *always* like Aunt Bea on the Andy Griffith show, but this is real life, not fiction. We always had freshly baked cookies after a game. Mrs. Eggert was quite a seamstress. Rarely did my Little League uniforms fit me when I was young. I was still in the husky stage. I also tore the knees out sliding and catching in a million games. Mrs. Eggert would repair and actually taper my uniforms on a routine basis. One year she started tailoring custom fit pants for me out of Lefty's old semi-pro uniforms. That tradition lasted for years. Mrs. Eggert is as honest as they come. Often Paul and I would come barging in and tell her of a tournament we were going to play in and that we needed a permission slip that day. She would drop everything and drive me down to William J. Schmitt Inc. where my father was the purchasing agent. Pretty soon this was happening more often. Mrs. Eggert soon became adept at scratching my father's name. Mrs. Eggert understood that you just had to do anything, for baseball.

The actual whiffle ball games took place in Paul's back yard. The strike zone encompassed the area of the back rest of an old upright tin lawn chair that rocked. The chair was light pastel green with faded off-white arms. The strike zone would include the arms because that pitch was on the knees! We made up rules and played for hours. The "whiffle" ball moved like crazy if you held it with the holes exposed and let go like a knuckle curve. This movement taught us never to take your eye off the ball.

Before long, we started playing with the plastic ball. I learned quickly that you had to start your breaking pitch eight to ten inches inside in order to nip the arm piece on the outside corner, at fifteen feet! I would envision Camillo Pascual on the mound, grip the ball down the seams, wind up slowly, deliver nearly right over the top and zap. At the point of release I could feel the friction between my finger and that raised seam and snap down as hard as I could. I had to ... because both Paul and Larry could really hit. Paul's fast ball would hop. This game taught us about bat speed with a snap at the end. Mrs. Eggert would stay quite busy settling arguments over cookies. I'm certain that Mrs. Eggert wanted to "be" the great arbiter Bill Klem!

Paul was already a heck of a pitcher. He started varsity games as a freshman. Like Catfish Hunter, Paul could really hit too. One day a few years later, when we were juniors in high school, Paul was complaining that his curveball just wasn't sharp enough. I promptly bought a new "raised seamer" and we found that same tin chair buried away in his parents' garage! That entire lesson stressed that feeling of the friction, on the point of release. Paul really never did master that curve but developed a slider like the other Catfish's. As a senior he pitched a no-hitter, one-hitter, two-hitter, and three-hitter in a row. I'm quite certain that he did not lose a game that season.

Paul always had a temperament to win, being a "Redhead." Once we were playing *Electric Football* at my house after school. We had quite an argument about where the player went out of bounds. Suddenly, **"POP,"** Paul swung and clocked me right in the eye! I hit the floor and was actually "out" for a few seconds. I was embarrassed (a guy thing) and hopped back on my feet. I wasn't sure what just happened. I was positive that Paul wanted to "be" Rube Marquard that day!

Paul moved back to Rochester for a few years after college and his Navy stint. We won three more City League Slow Pitch championships. He was the best first baseman that I ever threw to, from third base. I cannot remember him making even one error, and certainly saved me my share of them. But soon Paul switched careers and moved his family to the Washington DC area. We still rendezvoused with the Eggerts for vacations, meeting them on the Jersey shore. The only time that Paul ever disappointed me in his life, was when he showed up one year, and forgot his mitt! He remembered that he forgot it (Yogism), when he was two hours away from home and wanted to drive back and get it!

Years later when Paul was visiting his parents, he called me and told me the good news. Mrs. Eggert thought that there were some baseball cards still in their attic! I met Paul at his folks' house. When I walked in and Mr. Eggert was in the parlor on his favorite chair. He was well into his eighties now. The Red Wing game was on. I smiled and was immediately drawn back to those great childhood discussions. I asked Mr. Eggert how he was doing and gave the same answer as always, "I am not complaining, but I'm not bragging either."

Paul and I excused ourselves and scampered upstairs to the attic. We quickly started to comb the attic floor and soon found a shoe box with some cards. There was about three or four dozen. I held my breath, but to no avail. No Mickeys or Hanks, (who Paul wanted to "be"). There was a nearly mint Del Crandall and believe it or not (Bob Costas) a mint Pumpsie Green and Eli Gerba! That is the gospel truth.

I began glancing around the attic and saw a baseball bat leaning between the studs of the wall. I quickly walked over and saw that it was an old H&B hardball bat. I lifted it up for examination and looked at the barrel end above the trademark. The bat had been engraved with a magnifying glass. In large capital letters it read **MICKEY**. I quickly turned it over to check the knob end. Yes, there it was a "**7**" burned into the wood. I turned and asked Paul "what he was doing with *my* bat?" Obviously I had left it there 15-20 years ago. This time there was no argument or fight.

That was about the last time I saw Mr. Eggert. The bat episode was meant to be, and served as proper closure. I will pass the bat on to my children, but I'm not sure that

I can still "crank one" well over 400 feet!

This past spring I was driving by Monoco Oil co. where Garry Hurwitz is now the president of the family business. I wanted to say "hi" and make a quick "pit stop." Garry is forty-eight and still playing competitive organized hardball. He has been pitching for a few years, fulfilling a childhood dream. The name of his team is the Yankees. He then complained to me that he could not break off a real good curve. I guess Garry now wants to "be" David Cone! With my business suit on, we went outside and I started to explain the proper arm position, the proper point of release including the friction point on the seams and the snap. After about five to ten minutes, I stopped and told Garry that we needed just the right whiffle ball, a "raised seamer"! He looked at me a little weird. I wonder if Mrs. Eggert still has "homeplate"?

CHAPTER 9

Our Hero and Role Model

Today was a sad day, August 13, 1995. Mickey passed away today with dignity. Some of my great friends called with deep concern and hoping that I was going to take the news okay.

No one touched upon the chronology of baseball and exactly how and why his impact was so great, as we will discuss. I wholeheartedly disagree with everyone in the country who say that Mickey was always an idol but not an excellent role model. First of all, Mickey was not an alcoholic in his younger days. As Whitey Ford mentioned, "they picked their spots as to days off and drinking activities. "Mickey's heavier days arrived later in his career and after he retired. Nobody could have accomplished what he did on the field being in a drunken stupor. Even if they did carouse a bit they kept their private life to themselves. It is true that the "Ol' Perfesser" did call them "Whisky Slick" or "Slick" on occasion.

If Mickey wasn't a great role model why did this author and literally many millions of young men admire him and want to be just like him? Why was I so captivated at seven years old to be ripping the newspaper open at the end of 1956 to see if he would beat out Al Kaline for RBI and complete the winning of the Triple Crown? Think of his wonderful and profound influence of keeping a generation of baseball players on the fields, instead of the streets, from 8 o'clock in the morning until 5 at night. Everyone was practicing to become Mickey Mantle, all summer. Millions and millions of boys and men wanted to "be" Mickey Mantle.

If you ever walked into old Yankee Stadium you would get an instant tingling up your spine. On August 30, 1964 I arrived in New York City with the purpose of going to the World's Fair. Soon I discovered that the Yankees, who I had never seen live, would be home one more day and playing the Boston Red Sox! August 31, 1964 was the date that I had long waited for. My Uncle Sam instructed my father and me how to take the subway from Brooklyn to the Bronx. He only would go with us the next day to see the Mets! The subway was already a bit scary and we ran into a potential obstacle of a staggering drunk. We were alarmed, but a local lady quickly embarrassed the drunk back into place with her expert confrontation! Besides that small incident, the subway was uneventful. Soon my heart was pounding as I rushed up the ramp to catch my first glimpse of the playing field.

"This is the House That Ruth Built" was drooling from

my lips.

What a beautiful start to a vacation and the rest of my life. A few innings into the game Mickey got up with the bases loaded. The Stadium was filled with Yankee fans and went berserk. Then, approximately the same chill went up my spine. Batting left handed Mickey only fired a single, like it was shot out of a cannon. I was satisfied. I had never seen a ball hit that hard in all my life, nor could I even imagine the impact and strength of this human being. Of course the final score was in favor of the Yankees, 9-3. That was a great day.

After the game we were allowed to go onto the playing field and visit the monuments of Ruth, Gehrig and Huggins. Suddenly a thought passed through my mind "Oh my God, if I die now it wouldn't be so bad."

One reason that Mickey was simply the best and the last superstar by definition was that he could perform every aspect of the game better than anybody, even if in pain. That is what I call a *great* role model, hero and idol. Bob Costas captured your childhood within his eulogy when he clearly depicted that wonderful feeling - in between a bubble gum card of Eli Gerba and Pumpsie Green would lie the ultimate cherished prize, a mint Mickey Mantle card, hopefully without the residue of the pink, cheap-tasting, bubble gum, the kind that our dentists loved.

When Mickey inspired millions of young men to be the best you could be because of his performance, isn't that also a role model? So many would follow and not use injuries as an excuse to stop excellence, play in pain, drive to be the best in the clutch, act gracefully under pressure, and win gracefully. Mickey also gave awesome inspiration to his teammates, as Bobby Richardson commented about Mickey's return in 1963 and hitting a home run in Baltimore in his first bat as a pinch hitter, after breaking a bone in his foot. Inspiration is a wonderful quality that only a few could carry. That was a God-given attribute that Mickey possessed and really didn't understand. Fate dictated that he was not supposed to understand this fact and just be a clean-cut poor boy from Oklahoma. This blindness enhanced his ability to be a role model.

Mickey became a role model on the tangible plays on the field and the way he carried himself. This was amplified by his rate of success and his ability to win so many World Series, coveted awards and titles. He became an idol on the intangible psychology of winning and his All-American Golden Boy looks.

Mickey had the knack for producing in the clutch and winning like Ruth and DiMaggio. It would take pages of script to name all the heroic home runs of his career. A few come to mind such as the enormous homers off Stobbs, Ramos and Fischer, Game 2 of the 1953 World Series, the homer off Maglie for Don Larsen, the shot he called off Barney Schultz to win in the ninth inning in 1964, the 1963 homer in Baltimore after coming off the DL with a broken foot, one off the great Koufax in the 1963 World Series, and the one he "did the great Satchel some damage," even when DiMaggio could not. Mickey owns the World Series records for home runs (18), RBI (40), runs scored (42), walks (43), extra-base hits (26) and total bases (123). This led to winning 7 of 12 World Series. Now how was that not being a role model for his teammates and a whole generation of athletes?

Author David Halberstam, who has won every major journalistic award, including the Pulitzer Prize, commented about why Mantle was this enormous hero in his book *October 1964*. "Everything about Mantle seemed to come from a storybook about the classic American athlete: he was the modest country boy with a shock of blond hair that turned the color of corn silk during the summer, who became a superstar in the big city." I do believe that Mickey Mantle was put on this earth to play baseball and precisely at the time when he did play.

Mickey Mantle was paid that "unbreakable" American League ceiling of $100,000 for each of his last seven seasons. The first to earn that level was Hank Greenberg in 1947. DiMaggio, Williams and Musial also were at the ceiling. Koufax and Drysdale were ahead of their times in 1966. They held out together and wanted a three-year $1 million package deal for the two of them! Koufax settled for $125,000 up from $85,000. Drysdale settled for $115,000 up from $80,000. Mays earned $130,000 at the end of Mickey's career. The structure of salaries was very clear in both leagues. Not by coincidence, the leaders were Mantle, Mays and Koufax!

Mickey earned approximately 1.1 million dollars in his whole career. He retired after the 1968 season. He was the highest-paid player in the American League for at least those last seven seasons. His total value to a team was larger than anybody else. Mickey had no idea that Whitey and Yogi were only making about one half of his salary because that was certainly not talked about. It was a given that Mickey's salary was the highest in the American League and most often in all of baseball, and that's that. At today's prices Mickey acknowledged that he would have been a part owner.

Cal Ripken has just played in his record-breaking season. He is a good man and a good ball player. He has already earned more than 46 million dollars! The question is how did we get there and where will it end? The impact on the game may be suicidal for baseball.

CHAPTER 10

College, Writing and the Next Perfect Job

As a freshman in college we practiced the art of writing and self-expression. By this point in the book, it is clear that I would not be an eloquent writer if I lived another 100 years. My first inclination of this was that I completely understood Casey Stengel and for that matter Yogi when they spoke. Everyone thought Casey was nuts, but me. I was also allowed to stay up late one school night a week, because I enjoyed and understood the humor of Groucho Marx! For the record, I did not understand Jimmy Piersall but did understand Roberto Clemente, who would be sure to wear a sweatshirt on the hottest days! The only language that I am sure of is contained within *The Official Rule Book*. But I do love baseball and writing has given me the opportunity to express some keen observations.

One day Professor Fred Blomgren gave us <u>silent</u> work time in class to develop our themes of a current assignment. I had already completed the work. Lo and behold instead I inked my first poem. Line by line, I passed the poem to Roger, who was sitting next to me. Each of the four lines became more hilarious than the one before and tied-in slang expressions of our childhood. Upon completion Roger could hardly focus his eyes to read the lines. He was having a laughing jag during quiet time and wisely just got up and left the room. I stayed and was silent but the tears were streaming off my face and my shirt was soaked. Humor is a wonderful thing. Writing was not so bad after all! Fred Blomgren was the consummate gentleman and never mentioned this incident.

Most college kids need extra money and most all my friends were still in the same boat. Gary "Bubba" Snyder was a friend of mine and his father owned a small kosher style delicatessen for a few years. David was Mr. Snyder's name but very few people knew that. To the world he was known as **"CRISCO"** Snyder. Whenever anybody inquired about his unusual name, he would merely point to his butt and say "fat in the can"! Crisco's smile certainly resembled that of Babe Ruth's. Crisco was a superb left-handed athlete also, a great father and husband and the "Babe Ruth" of practical jokes.

The first time I met Crisco was when I was about fifteen. Upon opening his delicatessen I did not meet him right away. His store was always mobbed on Sunday mornings and I was busy either taking serious batting and fielding practice or bowling. About four months or so later, my father wanted to stop into Crisco's on a

Sunday, after I was already out practicing with Roger.

I thought about the crowd, which I was not fond of, but my father said it probably wouldn't be too bad by that time of day. In walked my father, myself and Vera, who would years later become my wonderful step-mother, in a "Kravetz doubleheader" ceremony. Yes that's correct, on December 20, 1969 the Kravetz family played two. Both Bernie and Maurine were married in successive ceremonies. I'm sure Ernie Banks would have been proud!

There were about fifteen people or so lined up by the meat counter. We quietly positioned ourselves behind the crowd six or eight feet away. Almost immediately Crisco looked up and our eyes met. He was cutting salami at a record pace on the meat-cutting machine. He looked down for a second and then back and started to smirk, in his beautiful boyish manner, and laugh at the same time. He then said above the whole crowd, **"You must be Bobby Kravetz, the catcher."** I simply said "yes." He immediately yelled **"then let's see you catch this"** and flung three salami slices at me in a row, through the crowd! I caught all three and he immediately yelled to Art, who was cutting lox, **He's good Art, he's good!"**

One day in college, Bubba informed me that the deli needed help and that Crisco wanted me to go down to the store for an interview. I wasn't sure that this was on the level and didn't respond for a few days. Soon Bubba approached me and said that Crisco really did need somebody. Bubba made me commit to going down for an interview.

I strolled into the store after a mid-afternoon class and nobody was there except Crisco and an employee named Rona. Rona worked a few hours a day when her children were in school. I got to know her because Bubba and I stopped in frequently for a six-pack, for our poker games. Rona was so nice, with a quick wit and had a wonderful sense of humor. Upon entering, Crisco's expression became <u>extremely</u> business-like. I had never seen that side of him before even when he was yelling at Bubba. I now felt highly apprehensive, as you would feel in all professional interviews. In a very solemn tone of voice, Crisco looked up and said "First I'll give you the psychological portion of your exam and then Rona will take you in back for your physical!" I immediately cracked up and Rona was already laughing a little. Crisco very sternly barked, **"What are you laughing for, this is a serious business."** I calmed down with Crisco's coaxing. He insisted that I fully concentrate and carefully listen to the one question that he was going to ask me. I was quiet and poised. Rona had strayed away not being able to take it any longer. He looked at me straight in the eye and asked me, "How many ounces are there in a pound?" I rose to the occasion like there were two outs in the bottom of the ninth and immediately responded, "Crisco, **there are exactly fourteen and one-half ounces in a pound!"** Crisco immediately yelled to Rona, **"GET HIM AN APRON!"**

Saturday and Sunday afternoons became a great education in life and baseball. Art, the meatcutter, soon found out that my baseball knowledge was only fair at best, when referring to baseball players of his generation. We discussed at length the careers of Pepper Martin, Marty Marion, Dizzy and Daffy Dean, Rabbit Maranville "Fat Freddie" Fitzsimmons, Ducky Medwick, Bill Terry George Sisler, Arky Vaughn, Bill Dickey, Stuffy McInnis, Mel Ott, Zack Wheat, Heinie Manush, the great "Shoeless

Joe" and Satchel. As soon as I would arrive Art would start with Kid Nichols, Joe Wood, Eppa Rixey, Bobo Newsom, Bobo Holloman, Pete Gray, Dummy Hoy, Addie Joss, "Vinegar Bend," Schoolboy Roe, Ferris Fain, Irish Meusel and hosts of others. He would just challenge me with his eyes protruding out of his head, and that stare! CRISCO and Art selected players that had unique nicknames, but none called "CRISCO." We debated Hall of Fame credentials and the like. I would be quizzed on knowing Babe Ruth, Lou Gehrig, Jimmy Foxx, Al Simmons, and Joe Cronin (Hubbell's successive strikeout victims in the '34 All-star game). I was quickly taught a most valuable lesson, that you better know your subject matter well if you're going to open your mouth. At that point I went to the library to read everything that I could get my hands on. They call this work?

Crisco and I became close friends and soon he was bowling with my father and me, on our team. You cannot imagine what it was like to hear nearly a new joke, per frame, for the whole year!

He ran a smart "business-like" store from an investment point of view. As a matter of fact, one of the most grueling and best debates that I have ever won in my life was over a twenty-cent raise, that put me up to two dollars per hour! But you also had to be on your toes at all times. *Every* day was April Fool's Day!

Once Crisco staged a robbery of his own store, just to shake up Rona. Before the plot was carried out, Crisco got nervous that Rona might not respond well under that circumstance. Crisco then tipped off Rona that Art was going to come into the store disguised as a stick-up man, with his finger in his pocket, simulating a gun. (Dark shades and a trench coat). Now the joke was on Art, as usual, who weighed 135 pounds ringing wet.

Crisco immediately hired a 6-foot, 4-inch, 245 pound or so customer to hide in the back room. Right on schedule, Art came in to do his skit, *not* knowing about the change of plot. As soon as he looked at Rona, handed her a bag and said, "Put the big ones in here," Crisco blasted a loud shrill, on a gym whistle. Jerry Jacobs came wheeling out of the back room, grabbed Art in two different spots and started doing military presses with him. Art was fearful for his life and **SCREAMING** for mercy ... Some of the customers in the store were terrified, others didn't even bat an eyelash!

One day Art, Crisco and I were standing together behind the counter when a gorgeous woman walked in, that we had never seen before. Art quickly started making conversation and dominating the moment. To this Crisco was **pissed**, because he was beat to the punch at his own game! Soon Crisco was burning and looking for his opening. Crisco knew that precious time was passing and he **had** to get the upper hand. Immediately Crisco moved to position himself face to face with Art, and started staring at him, as if he is ready to go jaw to jaw with the chief umpire. Crisco then abruptly cut into the conversation and loudly said, **"Art before you go any farther, I just want to push your eyeballs back into your head!"** and then went to manipulate Art's eyeballs! I laughed so hard that I had go into the back room for the next fifteen minutes!

Crisco has since passed away, but is with Bubba and me everyday. Crisco's ability to tell a joke will never be matched in quantity or quality. Thank God for my dear doctor friend Sidney Weinstein M.D., who has now filled this role with high honors. Sidney is sixty-two and looks like forty-five. Each year he asks me about the possibility of playing on our competitive softball team. I love optimistic people and Dr. Sid is fantastic. I never asked, but I imagine Sid wants to "be" Ernie Banks. Humor, baseball and life go together.

CHAPTER 11

The Evolution of Change

In 1968, Mickey's last year, he made $100,000. No other player deserved the same amount measured by relative skill of playing the game and reputation. No other player received more in the American League. The problem arose before June 8, 1969 which was Mickey Mantle Day at Yankee Stadium. Mickey went to spring training and decided that he just could not endure the pain and perform anymore. Who would be the next superstar? More accurately, who would be the best player left to dominate and or be the ambassador of baseball?

Without a doubt nobody could match Mickey's baseball prowess or presence. Should America embrace the next best home run hitter in an up-and-coming Reggie

Jackson, prolific singles hitter Pete Rose, an exceptionally gifted catcher, Johnny Bench, base stealers Maury Wills and Lou Brock, a pitcher who just won 31 games (Denny McClain), Don Drysdale, who ran off an incredible streak of 58 2/3 scoreless innings, or Curt Flood and Carl Yazstremski, who had a combination of skills? Could a pitcher dominate who was overpowering like Bob Gibson or a 22-year old Catfish who already hurled a perfect game and who could also hit! (Catfish was paid $5,000 extra by Finley for his hitting ability and went 3-4 in his perfect game-plus 3 RBI). Willie McCovey and Harmon Killebrew were the MVPs of 1969. Frank Robinson and Henry Aaron possessed great skills. Tom Seaver was already showing the world his greatness and led the Miracle Mets of 1969 to a world championship season. Steve Carlton had now struck out a record 19 in a game, but lost. The great race for the spotlight was now up for grabs because *nobody* could be Mickey Mantle.

Times were a-changing for America. Between the senseless assassination of John Kennedy and the equally senseless involvement in Vietnam, this new generation started to openly question public policy and there was an inherent mistrust of authority, which would never be restored to the "pure" and innocent fifties. The social structure of society and the salary structures were beginning to be torn down. Revolution was present on our college campuses and now in the minds of our people.

Salaries of the top players now ranged up to Bob Gibson making $85,000, Orlando Cepeda $80,000, and Roger Maris $75,000 in 1968. Close behind was Curt Flood at $72,500 and Lou Brock at $70,000.

"Flood was an interesting case and when offered

$77,500 by Augie Busch and the Cardinals, he wanted $90,000, proclaiming to be the best center fielder in the game. He demanded that he would take not a penny less. Mr. Busch gave in but this opened the floodgates for bitter future negotiations, an inherent mistrust on both sides. It was that brewing issue and strengthening of the powerless player's union, and yet another challenge of the "reserve clause" which in this case carried racial overtones, that made major change imminent. Flood was irked over being traded to the Phillies after the 1969 season and decided rather than to play, to sit out the entire season. His lawsuit against baseball went to the Supreme Court, where he ultimately lost a close decision with a 5-3 vote." It was viewed by many as a heroic action. He put himself out of baseball when he was still near his prime. Others could argue that it has led to chaos. I only ask the question could this have possibly happened when Mickey was still playing? I doubt it.

The "reserve clause" was not a new vehicle of bitterness between owner and player but yet can be traced back to the 1870s. "Around 1871 the first major league concept was formed. This establishment was called the National Association of Professional Baseball Players. It soon failed because there was no way to keep players from jumping from team to team. In 1876 the National League of Baseball Clubs was formed, putting the authority in the hands of the owners rather than the players. By 1879, the practice of putting several of the teams best players "on reserve" was practiced. No other team could or would sign these protected players. Soon the American Association was started and both leagues adhered to the protection policy of the reserve clause. The owners used the reserve clause to keep salaries down".

John Montgomery Ward was the star infielder of the New York Giants. He was also a law school graduate and instrumental in forming a players union which was named the Brotherhood of Professional Baseball Players. The objective of the union was to help negotiate higher salaries and clear up other restrictions. Interestingly, Ward was the first to refer to the reserve clause as a form of slavery; many of his contemporaries had fought in the Civil War.

Owners agreed to terms by Ward and the Brotherhood, but soon reneged. The Brotherhood was ready to strike. Instead they played the season with their "oppressive" contracts while gaining backers to promote a brand new league targeted in most every major National League city. The National proceeded to wipe out the American Association by attracting their best talent. In 1901 the American League was set up and went back to raid the National League. By 1902 a "peace treaty" was made between the two leagues. Some certainly would say that Mr. Ward was a hero.

The game rolled along pretty smoothly with the exception of the new Federal League of 1914-1915, that tried and successfully raided some of the premier baseball stars, but was soon to be short lived. Tyrus Raymond Cobb was ruling the American League, but had his equal in the National in Honus Wagner. George Herman Ruth was arguably the best pitcher in the league. The first five times that he faced the great Walter Johnson, who was in his prime, Ruth beat Johnson. This included games of scores of 4-3,5-1,2-1,1-0 in thirteen innings and 2-1. He wasn't too shabby of a hitter either!

It is said that "all dark clouds have a silver lining". There was a dark cloud looming over baseball in 1919.

The Black Sox were about to mar the cleanliness of our pure American pastime. This led to two definite outcomes. One was created for "the good of the game", and the other, which was the silver lining, by fate!

In November of 1920, Judge Kenesaw Mountain Landis of the United States District Court as arbitrator, a one-man court of last resort, was named the first Commissioner of Baseball. Baseball had just been rocked by the "Black Sox" scandal and it was felt that its governing three-man National Commission didn't have the capabilities to restore baseball's good name. Landis had previously presided over the court case involving the Federal League and didn't make a decision for eleven months. The Federal League, which needed a sweeping decision to stay in business, settled for a cash settlement and folded. Landis' term was for at least seven years. The headline in the *New York Times* actually read: BASEBALL PEACE DECLARED; LANDIS DECLARED DICTATOR. I guess that this was all for "*the good of the game!*" I didn't realize that baseball was played in Russia too. Maybe Ed Cicotte and friends changed the game more than anybody else. I wonder if John Montgomery Ward was still alive by some miracle, in 1919-1920. If so, he would have probably dropped dead on the spot.

Baseball survived under Judge Landis' iron fist for many years without major changes. Landis asserted his power and showed everyone that he would and did take the upper hand, even against the great Babe Ruth. Landis forbade Ruth to go on any more postseason barnstorming tours. Ruth was his own man and also making a lot of money by playing these extra games said that Landis could "go jump in a lake". Landis responded by suspending Ruth for the first forty games of the 1922 season! At least Ruth was seen playing in his prime, by many other cities for a few years, including Rochester, N.Y. and Mr. Eggert.

Actually one could argue that the next largest change was 1947 when Jackie Robinson broke the "color barrier". Finally, but slowly, did the owners "buy-in" to a change that finally **would be**, for the good of the game.

Interestingly, Dandy Gardella, a Giant outfielder, had jumped to the short-lived Mexican League in 1946 and had been blacklisted from baseball in the United States! He sued baseball and challenged the reserve clause. He won the first round in court, and baseball quickly settled out of court!

In 1953 a minor leaguer named George Toolson sued baseball for violation of antitrust laws. The Supreme Court upheld the 1922 decision that stated that baseball was not covered by antitrust laws, by Chief Justice Oliver Wendell Holmes. "Toolson was stuck in the Yankee organization behind well-stocked teams." This Court decision played nicely right into the Yankee owners' hands, in the exact time of Mickey's budding career. Now all the owners together would enforce the rigid salary structure built around Mickey's salary and prowess on the field. This could not and would not change until Mickey retired and Marvin Miller found the wedge. Mickey was the benchmark of performance in a tightly woven salary structure.

Marvin Miller was said to change the game as much as anyone including Babe Ruth or John Montgomery Ward. Miller was born in 1917 and grew up in Brooklyn near Flatbush Avenue and rooted for "dem Bums". Miller had graduated from NYU, with a BA in Economics, at nineteen. When he was working for the New York City

Welfare Department, he joined his first union and sat on his local's grievance committee. Soon after World War II broke out, Miller joined the National War Labor Board. It was there, that he was trained in the art of arbitration dealing with labor disputes. In 1950 he joined The United Steelworkers of America, and headed up their Human Relations Research Committee. Miller stayed there until 1965 and left as the powers of the union were changing.

Miller was elected the executive director of the Players Association in 1966. He soon worked hard to gain the confidence of the players which was no easy task. The players had a 100-year-old mind set with regards to changing the "business of the game", with few exceptions. At first he had almost a total vote off "no confidence"! Immediately Miller began to visit each and every player in spring training camps and at games. He talked about incremental changes in areas of wages, improved working conditions and better benefits. By 1968 he was to complete a collective bargaining agreement. This agreement was to be said to be the first ever negotiated in any sport! Miller was the master of incremental change and the negotiation process.

In 1969 negotiations were going on with few promising results. He boldly suggested that no player sign his 1969 contract until a benefit plan agreement had been reached. Miller needed desperately to gain support and was now in need of a trump card. Mickey Mantle was indeed that card. Miller asked Mickey for his vote of confidence, which would carry an overwhelming influence with his peers. During spring training of 1969 Mickey knew that he had to retire. He could no longer take the pain and produce as expected. Steve Hamilton, the Yankees' player representative, requested of Mickey, that he not announce his retirement until after his endorsement of the Players Association be known. The only thing that Mickey asked was "if the results would be good for the players?" Mickey agreed that the MLBPA could use his name. His *official* position was announced that he would not sign his 1969 contract, until the negotiation sessions had yielded an acceptable agreement of the pension plan.

So even as Mickey's knees were crumbling and could not be that idol and hero on the field, he still had a major influence on the immediate fate of the players. It would be interesting to explore a little different scenario. What if Mickey could still play his game at this time and was against the Player's Association? Would change have come so fast? Would Marvin Miller even gain full support, or be ousted as executive director? The lords of control could have, at this point, still catapult back into history. We could have seen Mr. Peabody and Sherman going *way back*, 100 years to the era of Montgomery Ward, but more likely to 1920 with Judge Landis.

CHAPTER 12

<u>Times of Revolution and Peter M. Seitz</u>

Stories of individual heroes were certainly written during the period immediately after Mickey's retirement. "Tom Terrific", Fergie Jenkins who played in "the sandbox", Bob Gibson, Steve Carlton, Gaylord Perry, Wilbur Wood, Frank and Brooks, Al Kaline, Rod Carew, Joe Torre, Harmon Killebrew, Willie McCovey, Roberto, Bench, Rose and so many others took the spotlight. But soon there was a lot of concentration on articles involving a miracle team. Could it be that the "amazing" Mets of 1969 happened with a "higher game plan" for the good of the game? As the banner read in the stands, "You've Gotta Believe!" With the amazing Mets carrying the interest of baseball we were still looking for the "new

Mickey" or the next perfect team.

Jim Palmer, along with Mike Cuellar and Dave McNally, Mickey Lolich, and Vida Blue were battling Catfish Hunter to be the best pitcher in the American League. Andy Messersmith became a twenty-game winner in 1971. Brooks and Frank were at their peak and so was Roberto. The truth of the matter is that there were now so many very good players, all who were about equal in value, to their teams. Now the "Big Red Machine" was getting oiled up for a smooth run. Rose, Bench, Perez, and Morgan were the "new superstars".

In 1970 Flood vs. Kuhn came to trial. Flood was a courageous man to give up so much in his prime. He also had to "go it alone" or at least without the overwhelming support of the players. It was a close case losing 5-3 with one abstention, in favor of Kuhn and the "Lords" of the game. Bob Short, owner of the Senators, had offered Flood a contract before the case was heard by the Supreme Court, with the salary of $100,000! This exemplifies that the salary ceiling was now broken, as Mickey had retired and Willie Mays was near the end of his career. After a brief try, Flood called it quits. It was obvious that the preparation and the strain of his challenging the reserve clause had taken its toll.

In 1972 the Player's Association wanted to negotiate the benefit plan. When both sides could not agree on the issues, the Player Representatives of each team voted 21-4 in favor of a strike! The MLBPA voted 663-10 (with two abstentions) to authorize a strike! The players wanted an increase of $500,000 in their pension fund, due to raising costs of about that same amount per year, since 1969, their last negotiated settlement. The strike lasted 13 days, and all 86 lost games would not be made up.

Marvin Miller was surprised at the willingness of the Players Association to strike! But everything could not have been going better for the cause. First he gained the position of executive director of the Player's Association, which allowed him to negotiate with the owners and scrutinize the player's contract language. Next he gained a vote of confidence from the players with Mickey's backing. Then baseball had no true superstar and the best players were spread throughout the teams of each league. Salaries started escalating due to the "new" superstar relativity. In 1972 Hank Aaron made $200,000! Following that Miller discovered that the players were willing to "revolt" together (strike) vs. separately (Flood).

By 1972 through 1974 we saw the great Oakland A's win three World Series in a row. They were marvelous teams with so many great role players, not unlike the roles and platoon system that Casey Stengel used with so much success. Casey had learned that system from the great John McGraw of the Giants. Oakland had nobody that was the equal of Mickey, but many who would could challenge for the now opened dominating position. Together the A's had synergy and learned how to win together and sometimes how to fight each other. Fingers fought with Odom, Reggie went toe to toe with North as Fosse got caught in the middle and got a disc in his neck crushed!

Bert Campanaris was an All-Star, Joe Rudi was darn good and a great team player, Sal Bando was great in the clutch, Billy North was speedy, Vida Blue, Kenny Holtzman, and Catfish were the best tandem around, not to mention the efforts of "Blue Moon Odom", and then relieved by Mr. Fingers! Gene Tenace and Mike Epstein hit key home runs and drove in clutch runs. There was also a very athletic, and very driven kid, named Reggie!

It bothers me when people tell me that Catfish Hunter was a "true" free agent. It points out that too many people do not really know the facts around baseball but insist that they do and are experts. (Too often Little League arguments are based on notions of people that do not even know the rules, let alone the proper interpretation.) Hunter was declared a free agent due to a breach of contract by A's owner Charles Finley. He was not the benefactor of the years of stress that Curt Flood toiled at, in order to try to break the "reserve clause". Andy Messersmith and Dave McNally were the first two "pure" free agents. Actually I think that *A Whole Different Ball Game*, by Marvin Miller should be required reading, for all baseball fans!

Jim "Catfish" Hunter was certainly a premier pitcher of his times. He was also an excellent hitter, hitting .350 in 1971, going 36 for 103, and a slugging average of .408! On May 8, 1968 Hunter also went 3-4 when he pitched his perfect game and drove in 3 runs! But he was a premier pitcher. His slider owned the black of the plate, which is really a misnomer. Catfish lost a toe in a hunting accident when he was young. His silver lining came through this unexpected event. I submit that it was this slight physical abnormality that changed the pivotal point on the mound from the norm

Think about it this way. "Three Fingers" Brown caught his hand in a corn grinder when he was seven-years-old. He soon found out that he could put a good spin on the ball off the stub of his damaged forefinger! He became a very tough pitcher with a Hall of Fame career including a .649 winning percentage! Mordecai Brown had a phenomenal 1.04 ERA in 1906, the second best ever (Dutch

Leonard .98, 1914) and 1.31 ERA in 1909. Most experts of pitching will say that you throw with your legs, and the arm merely follows. Brown had a normal base with his feet, followed a peculiar angle of spin off his mutilated forefinger. Catfish had an abnormal base angle and this was accentuated by his arm extension. Both Brown and Hunter had their accidents early in life and learned how to pitch with their deformities. Had they learned "normally" and then forced to change due to an accident, the results would have most likely been career threatening. If you think that this is nonsense, go ask the followers of the great Dizzy Dean.

The great Dizzy Dean suffered a broken toe in the 1937 All-Star game. Earl Averill slammed a line drive off Dean's foot. Dizzy tried to come back before the toe was fully healed and never regained his top form.

In 1974 Catfish had signed a two-year contract with the eccentric Charles O Finley and the Oakland A's. He was paid the majestic salary of $100,000. "One provision of Hunter's contract called for one-half of his salary was to be paid to an insurance company, named by Hunter, for the purchase of an annuity. The money was to be paid in installments each payday during the season. Hunter gave Finley the name of the insurance company and Finley did not make a payment during the 1974 season!"

This clearly portrayed the old feudalistic attitude of the owners. Finley was informed in writing of his violation. He had ten days to respond to the charge. Marvin Miller points out in *A Whole Different Ball Game* that "the Player may terminate this contract upon written notice to the Club" if there is no response within the ten days. Actually Miller states that this default and termination clause had been in all Uniform Player's Contracts for upwards of forty years! It was not surprising that the headstrong Finley tried at that point to simply pay to Hunter what he owed as a mere oversight and blow it off! Hunter's lawyer informed not to take a cent at that point. His case was heard and the arbitrator, Peter M. Seitz, upheld Hunter's claim to being a free agent. An important point of the decision mentioned by union boss Marvin Miller that "Seitz remedy was specifically derived from the language of the contract itself."

This decision to a fan was shocking, because although times were-a-changing, it was too *far out!* Still the decision did not have the same psychological impact of what was to soon come. Fans felt very happy for Catfish because he was a class guy who deserved to get away from Finley's authority. What the heck, Catfish owed him nothing and delivered three straight world championships with arm as well as his bat, and a little help from his friends! Besides, Munson soon called "King" George and insisted that Hunter would be the key to the future. Catfish, Reggie, and Munson would soon teach the Yankees how to win under pressure. Nothing could be better, except finding that "way back" machine of Mr. Peabody's.

Marvin Miller states in his book the following scenario of events that are here paraphrased. Miller realized in 1974 that a club had the right to renew a player's contract forever. Out of the Flood case came the agreement that "either party shall have the right to reopen the negotiations on the issue of the reserve system". Miller then decided to fight the reserve clause in the court not at the negotiating table. Miller wanted to test whether a club had the right of a contract renewal lasted forever or only existed for one additional year.

For you trivia buffs, in 1972 Ted Simmons played for the St. Louis Cardinals for one half of a season, without having signed a new contract. As a fan I can personally remember that I felt proud of Simmons as he went through this period. Sparky Lyle had more gumption, and pitched for the Yankees nearly the whole season before signing a 1973 contract! In 1974 Bobby Tolan went down to the wire, playing for the Padres before signing on the last day!

In 1974 Messersmith wanted a "no-trade" clause or provision included in a contract. Messersmith refused to sign his contract and played out the entire season, playing under a renewed contract. "In 1975 Messersmith pressed for the no-trade provision once again. Mr. O'Malley said, "Can't do it. The league wouldn't approve the contract."! Miller called the statement "absolute bull". Miller wanted to see how many successive renewed contracts could be given to the same player. Miller also checked the records and found out that Dave McNally was the only other unsigned player."

McNally was an interesting case because he started the season with Montreal and then left baseball because of his ineffective pitching. Miller asked McNally if he could "add his name to the grievance as insurance, if Messersmith decided to sign a new Dodger contract." McNally agreed. Miller and the Player's Association filled two grievances on the last day of the 1975 season.

Peter M. Seitz was the arbitrator that had ruled in Catfish Hunter's favor. Miller also points out that Seitz gave his opinion as the arbitrator in the National Basketball Association and the NBA Player's Association. The California Court of Appeals gave NBA star Rick Barry the right to sign with the Oakland Oaks of the ABA after playing out his option with the San Francisco Warriors. The NBA's Uniform Player's Contract was nearly the identical language as baseball's! That opinion became **the** key mind set for baseball.

Seitz stuck to his assignment of merely interpreting the contract. Commissioner Kuhn and the owner's argued on other grounds. On December 23, 1974 Seitz ruled that Messersmith and McNally were free to negotiate and sign with other teams! Seitz was fired as Marvin Miller signed the document, but the decision was upheld by Judge John W. Oliver. Soon after came the actual modification of the reserve rules, strikes, and lock outs by the owners.

What a feeling as a die-hard baseball fan! It was as if one day that you were mandated to throw out your life long rule book, and start all over with a foreign set of rules. I can distinctly remember that even after the decision that I expected it to be overturned by Judge Oliver. It was just too drastic of a change and nearly incomprehensible, with regards to predicting the new future of baseball, with so many potential implications. On one hand I felt real happy for the players. I do strongly believe in freedom of enterprise, and economics had just been a large piece of my formal education. On the other hand, it was clear what might and did evolve, as the rich would tend to get richer. Soon I began to accept this new reality. I realized that I could not solve the problems of the baseball world. Now the Yankees had a good chance to improve themselves after Mickey's retirement and a dismal stretch, that I was not able to identify with. I was already "in love" with the Hunter (23 wins, 328 innings) to Munson combination. Here I again learned a lesson in life, just tell me the rules and I will play the game!

CHAPTER 13

<u>Madison Ave.</u>   1977

RRRRING...

"Who's there?"

"This is Munson, who the hell is this?"

"This is *Mr.* Steinbrenner, Thurman."

"Sorry George, whatcha want?"

"Who's around ... Thurman?"

"Well there's Me, and Roy, Nettles and Sparky."

"How about if you guys take off tomorrow?" You know that Hilton, Homecoming luncheon."

"Sure Boss, that's great, see ya later!"

"Wait Thurman ... don't mind the press!"

"Aw come on, not me again?!"

"It's you turn Thurman, and remember if you want that large contract, we need large crowds!"

"We're doing all right."

"We were just behind our goal last year. We need a little more dissension and ... publicity."

"Sure Boss....but take it easy on me this time. When are we going fishing?"

The Power of Madison Avenue

I suppose I started to write baseball articles in 1977, to help express different feelings, observations and opinions of this new reality. Maybe writing was just the ticket that I needed to capture the moment, and once again savor the winning atmosphere, that had *finally* returned to the Yankees, in 1976. Okay, there was no Mickey, but by that age I fully realized that there never would be. Besides, I was becoming critical of clubhouse feuds that may hurt the chances of the Yankees winning, along with television announcers and too many statistics, "for the good of the game".

Indeed the rules of this era changed. There was now a strikingly new emphasis on "selling" the game vs. reporting on the game. This may in part have been due to the press having so much to exploit with each new blockbuster free agent. It was also necessary to do more selling to keep up with sky rocketing salaries. Attendance needed to rise proportionately. Television would follow and often over dramatize the results or the importance of the game.

One opening weekend of a season, I'm not sure which one, I was watching a game and Curt Gowdy was announcing. During that game he stated that "this was a critical inning, of a critical game, of that season." I turned the TV off. I'm not so sure that I have fully turned it back on since. Howard Cosell admitted that he had never played the game. He needed not to mention that fact. It was quite evident from his commentary. Often I watch without sound because so many announcers have "million dollar" voices, with little to back it up. Actually I still like to listen on radio and use my imagination, and draw my own mental images, as if I were back in the "transistor days".

On radio the announcers are quite often in the Hall of Fame, and also have a tendency not to talk so much. The insecure TV announcer doesn't realize that the game is a thinking game and will sell itself, if allowed. Besides there are too many in the TV booths. Each have their own agenda to follow to prove their worth, which often detracts. I did always enjoy Bill White and Rizzuto, and Kubek because they know the game, and have real insight. Jim Kaat has been involved at the highest level for so long and obviously so have Timmy McCarver and Jim Palmer. Vin Scully has it all and many had enjoyed

Red Barber in his day. If the Redhead was still announcing, I'm not sure he would have missed the amusing vignette that follows.

Nearing game 2,000 of Gehrig's great streak of 2130 consecutive games, there was one day when Gehrig just could not get out of bed! In those days, the general manager of the home team had the right and responsibility of calling off the games due to inclement weather. Ed Barrow was the GM at the time, of the Yankees. With *a* cloud in the sky, he called the game off! A brash young reporter, asked "Mr. Barrow, you didn't really think that it was going to rain, did you?" To this Barrow barked, "You're damn right I did...and besides......he'll be able to go tomorrow!"

I mention this great story for two reasons. First of all it is a great story and true. Secondly, we have just witnessed the passing of the great mark with Ripken's amazing streak. Nowhere in a sports column or TV and radio was there talk of Gehrig's day in bed, that I am aware of. I just happened to be in Baltimore during that week and read both the *Baltimore Sun* and *The Washington Post* and there was no mention of this, unless I just missed it. The point is that statistics are necessary to evaluate the past. When the batter is in the batter's box, statistics draw away from the beauty of the game and the moment. More baseball minds and baseball stories are needed to tie the past and the present together.

George Steinbrenner became the principal owner of the Yankees in January of 1973. The purchase price was about $10 million. George was hungry to build a winner. The Yankees were already improving with Thurman Munson now emerging as the team leader. In 1973-1975 Munson won the Gold Glove Award for being the best defensive catcher in the league. He could block the plate with the best of them, pounce on a bunt like a cat, and could throw out a runner from any position, especially if it was a critical runner. Munson had won The Rookie of The Year Award in 1970. In the pre-Hunter era, Munson already had hit over.300, but his best results were yet to come. The Yankees finished second to the Orioles in 1974 by just two games. Hunter was shopping around, after he was declared a free agent, and getting tired of playing that game versus baseball. "On the morning of New Year's Eve, 1974, he met with Clyde Kluttz of the Yankees and came to an agreement written on a paper napkin." The total was for $3.5 million! With this Hunter turned down better offers from the Padres and the Royals.

Quickly I realized that the new rules of the business of baseball weren't so bad if you lived in a large market, and there was a rich aggressive owner. I may not have liked this new morality, but the Yankees were meant to win. Without Mickey it would take more of a team effort.

In 1976 Munson was coming into his prime and Catfish was winning ball games. They took first place and beat the Royals in dramatic fashion in the League Championship Series, with a Chris Chambliss home run in the bottom of the ninth inning of the final game, with the score tied. That was a great feeling. It had been too long.

Now it was time to play the well oiled "Big Red Machine" in the World Series, with Sparky Anderson at the helm. Munson got at least one hit in every single game and more hits than anyone else in the Series. The Yankees lost because they didn't have the killer instinct that the Reds did. Anderson turned around and embarrassed Thurman with a statement about Munson's inability of competing, on the same level, with the great Johnny Bench. Munson had just hit .529 and Bench had hit .533. Oh excuse me! Maybe that day Munson wanted to "be" Sandy Koufax after a loss. Munson then swore that he or the Yankees would never be humiliated again with such nonsense.

Munson was named captain of the Yankees in the spring of 1976. He was the first named since the "Iron Horse," Lou Gehrig, held the title! In thirty post season games in his career, Munson averaged .357! That was third highest of all time. In World Series play he averaged .373! George was also rubbed the wrong way by Anderson's comments and was determined to do something about it his way, through free agency.

George soon thereafter lost Bobby Grich to Gene Autry and the Angels in a free agency battle, and now was to go after Reggie in New York City and swept him off his feet. He appealed to Reggie's inner ego of the life style that "King Reggie" deserved! George was persistent and wouldn't take no for an answer. Reggie said, "George hustled me like a broad."

Through the 1976-1978 era the Yankees were back on top of their game and became World Champions in 1977 and 1978. There were dramatic comebacks and homers by Chambliss and Dent, who were also steady with their gloves. Watching Nettles at third was as poetic as listening to Robert Frost and watching Brooks Robinson. In 1975 Nettles set a Yankee fielding record with a .975 percentage. In game three of the '78 Series he turned the tide with an ongoing spectacular performance. Nettles also hit numerous clutch homers including the final game of the '78 LCS.

Mickey Rivers was on a hot streak with his bat and

improved his fielding, by getting rid of the ball quicker to hold more runners. Munson and Reggie not only accomplished what they needed to on the field, but were the driving psychological force that wouldn't be denied victory. Reggie did his Ruth imitation in the 1977 World Series. (Most HRs 5-including his "three-fer", most total bases 25, most runs 10, slugging average record for a six game Series of 1.250, homered in his last four official at bats!) Randolph had a habit of coming up with the big play and hit. Piniella was a "gamer" and there was always the presence of the great Catfish, followed by Sparky or Goose. Dick Tidrow was so dependable as a set-up man and long reliever. Dent was the 1978 Series MVP and little Brian Doyle filled in for Randolph, who was injured with a torn hamstring, and hit .438! Naturally, Catfish won the last game (game 6) with the masterful Munson calling the signals. Guidry, undoubtedly, was the real MVP of all baseball in 1978, with a 25-3 record.

In 1980 the Kansas City Royals finally beat the Yankees in the LCS. In 1981 the Yankees returned to the World Series, and unfortunately lost to the Dodgers. Winfield amassed just one hit in the Series and George named him "Mr. May". But there was still a winning atmosphere among Yankee fans.

Meanwhile George Steinbrenner was making mega bucks on the TV rights of the Yankees. A record 76 million viewers had watched Boston lose the seventh game of the 1975 World Series. The Yankees were now again winning and picking up viewing steam. In the next ten years 40 million homes would have cable TV installed. In 1983 George sold his rights to the SportsChannel for $6.7 million a year. It granted the service of one hundred

Yankee games per season for the fifteen years. After five years George could buy out the remainder of his contract for $16 million.

In 1986, I was having lunch with my life long friend Gary Robinson. Gary is an amazing person. He was an excellent athlete in high school and college with football being his game, but always has loved baseball too. Gary is the entrepreneurial type with great vision and has developed many successful businesses. He understands people.

Gary and I were having a discussion about the business of baseball, TV, the Yankees, and George Steinbrenner. He told me that I should write to George and "tell him about your passion for the Yankees and your creative abilities and talents. Tell him of your energy level and that you're the 'Pete Rose of the pharmaceutical business.'" Gary *does* have quite a creative mind! But Gary and I are like brothers, and the lunch was great. The next day I formulated the letter.

I stated that I had a better marketing technique for the Yankees, and that I was interested in heading up the initiative. Essentially I outlined a marketing effort to enhance the Yankees' image, and take advantage of their rich tradition of Yankee Pride and winning. I suggested that the idea focused around showing vignettes of the past of Mickey, Lou, Yogi, Babe, Joe D., Roger, Whitey, Thurman, Reggie etc. on a regular basis between innings and I also begged for an interview.

The reply arrived post marked November 26, 1989, Bronx, NY. In a nut shell, the response dated November 24th, was a "Dear John" letter. I certainly doubt if it had ever gotten to George.

By the next year enhancements of the Yankees and

101

that Yankee Pride began on a regular basis. For the record, I am sick of court room trials on TV. Of course I'm just joking about a law suit, so I hope that George (or M. David Weildler, the 1986 Administrative Vice President-Treasurer) will read the FFAB chapter of this book. To top off the bad news was the fact that I didn't even get George's signature for my collection.

In 1988 MSG (Madison Square Garden Network) and SportsChannel squared off and battled each other after Steinbrenner had exercised his buy-out clause. MSG won the battle and agreed to pay a whopping $486 million. George also received a 5% bonus from the limited partners that were so delighted. George also arranged a $100 million sweetheart loan to the partnership group, secured by TV money. George received, as a 55-percent owner, 55-percent of the $100 million deal.

Statistics are overdone in live reporting of baseball today. Quite often they are used as a crutch to try to enhance a superficial understanding of the game. They do have their shortcomings and they also have a place of value, that being in quantifying and benchmarking the past.

Author Leonard Koppett says "Statistics are the life-blood of baseball." (*The New Thinking Fan's Guide To Baseball*.) He also discusses the main fallacies of statistics as outlined here:

1) Statistics can not be used to predict.

2) Statistics can not be used to prove a point. They can *convince* but can only prove the event that they record, not something else about it.

3) Statistics can be used to compare, "other things being equal", which they are not!

102

Statistics are great for baseball junkies and debates about the past. Author Bill James has written a great book, *The Politics of Glory*, which is a valiant attempt to restore some rhyme or reason about Hall of Fame Selections. He is also a master of baseball statistical analysis. The Society For American Baseball Research is the most wonderful organization. Without the efforts of that organization and books like *Total Baseball*, and the like, it would be nearly impossible to write a quality book or publication about baseball, without spending an inordinate time researching. In *Insider's Baseball*, L. Robert Davids, editor, explores many different methodologies and analyses that take a closer look at the players and their value.

"The base-out percentage is founded on the simple theory that a batter may embark on two journeys after completing a plate appearance: back to the dugout or, more pleasurably, the magic trek around the bases." The base-out percentage is calculated in the following manner: *Bases* are derived by adding total bases, walks, times hit by pitch, stolen bases, sacrifice hits, and sacrifice flies. *Outs* are derived by adding "outs batted" (at bats minus hits), sacrifice hits, sacrifice flies, times caught stealing, and double plays grounded into. Bases are then divided by outs. The result is base-on percentage. The idea is obviously to try to calculate how valuable of an offensive player really was.

For those with more than 3,000 bases, of past stars, **Mickey's career rated second of all time, with 6,472 bases and 5,547 outs and B-OP of 1.097.** Only Ted Williams was more effective with a BOP of 1.253 lifetime. Ted also was clearly not the fielder of Mickey. The moral of the story is that with interesting analysis as such, who could not like both baseball and statistics to a degree. The problem is timing of using statistics.

Baseball is like life in that nobody can predict the future, albeit every true fan has most likely had a premonition. Each at-bat is a new experiment. The intriguing fact is that one never *knows* what may happen, against all odds, on any given day, at-bat or play! There is even a chance that a pitched ball will hit the bat and go for a game winning base hit! Baseball is also rich in tradition and like life can bind one generation to another.

CHAPTER 14-1

The Real MVP of 1978
Originally scripted December, 1978
Updated 1995

This chapter must start with the old proverbial question: can a pitcher by the MVP of the league? The answer should be as fundamental as asking if the pitcher played in the league that year, and was extraordinary in his performance. The MVP IS NOT named the "MVP for NON-PITCHING PLAYERS." Why do critics say that a pitcher cannot be the MVP? Who wrote the criteria with an asterisk, Ford C. Frick? On the other hand, why should a pitcher be named MVP without extraordinary impacting his team's performance, but by merely doing something in the pitching category? There is a fine line here. Pitchers get paid to win games and their statistics reflect this fact more than non-pitchers.

In 1963 Sandy Koufax was named the MVP of the National League. Henry Aaron had an excellent year, but clearly was not the equal of Sandy's feats. Koufax went **25-5**, for a winning percentage of .833 and an amazing 311 innings. He gave up 214 hits, pitched **11** shutouts, posted an ERA of **1.88** and struck out **306** batters! Without this effort, the Dodgers would not have won the pennant, unless they had reincarnated Walter Johnson.

"Hammering Hank" hit his usual 44 home runs, with 130 RBI, scored 130 runs, hit .319 for average, and his slugging average was .586. Henry was the epitome of effectiveness. Koufax was Superman!

The real MVP of the American League and of all baseball in 1978, most certainly was "Louisiana Lightning" Ron "Gator" Guidry. I'm taking nothing away from Jim Rice and this is also not a "Yankee thing."

Rice had complained about not being named MVP in 1977 and the sports writers carried the sentiment over a bit. The writers "gave back" somewhat of a close call. Apparently they did not want to be Mr. Bill Klem (considered to be the best umpire ever). Rod Carew was the 1977 MVP and deserved it by hitting .388 with having also the rest of the necessary stats. Rice argued now for a later call that he did not deserve.

Let's take a look at the real impact of the 1978 seasons for both Rice and the "Gator":

The line on Rice reads:

G	AB	Hits	HR	R	Ave	TB	SA	Ks	Won Div
163	677	213	46	121	.315	402	.600	126	Lost to Guidry

Analysis:
A lot of at-bats

213 hits is very good but not great

46 HRs is real good but not in the mighty 50 club

121 runs is real good

402 bases is real good but the record is 457

.600 is darn good but not a Hall of Famer

126 Ks is a bust to keep rallies going

163rd game loss to Guidry is the **"knock out"** punch

The line on Guidry:

W	L	PCT.	GS	CG	IP	H	BB	Ks	ShO	ERA	Playoff
25	3	**.893**	35	16	274	18	772	24	**9**	**1.74**	**Winner**

Facts:

• Guidry won his first thirteen games to even keep the Yankees competitive

• **Guidry stopped an amazing 14 losing streaks. That is the major factor why he was the true MVP!**

• Struck out 18 Angels in one game

• 248 Ks in 35 starts is a great ratio

• **.893 IS THE HIGHEST WINNING PERCENTAGE IN BASEBALL HISTORY, FOR ANY STARTER, WITH AT LEAST 20 DECISIONS!**

• He beat Rice when all the chips were on the table

For the 1978 season Guidry was Koufax!

CHAPTER 14-2

The Great Captain
AUG '79

Like Williams, Clemente, Mantle and Maris he was misunderstood. Thurman Munson was often misunderstood because he was a general semanticist. He abstracted events at different levels than most! Instead of talking about what he did best, being so aware of miscommunications, he let his actions clearly show the world.

He was the best clutch hitter of his era including the great Rose. His psyche was higher than anyone since Mantle and Berra. His leadership was shown pragmatically, like Gehrig.

He was beautiful in an ironic sense like Yogi ... a bit dumpy but actually fast, at one time. People labeled him belligerent, only because they misconstrued his inner drive and confidence, to play the best that he could, regardless of injuries, like Mickey.

Captain Munson emulated "Yankee Pride" in the foot steps of Ruth, Gehrig, DiMaggio, and Mantle.

CHAPTER 14-3

<u>The Irony of Number 60!</u>
written in 1981

60! That magic number. The one that Babe wanted so much! He pranced around the bases yelling "Sixty, count 'em sixty! Let's see some other SOB match that!" But it was that blast off Tom Zachary on the last day of the season that distorted too many Americans' perception of baseball history. Number sixty distorted Ruth's finest season of 1921 into second place! It also distorted the lives of Tom Zachary, Roger Maris and Ford C. Frick. Unfortunately it gave the unsophisticated American public a nice and easy round number to remember!

This may have been Ruth's finest moment but not his finest season! A comparison of 1921 and 1927 clearly shows:

Year	G	AB	R	Hits	2B	3B	HR	BB	RBI	TB	AVE	SA	OB
1921	152	540	**177**	204	44	16	**59**	**144**	**170**	**457**	.378	**.846**	**.512**
1927	151	540	**158**	192	29	8	**60**	**138**	164	419	.356	**.772**	**.487**

1921 highlights also show that:

177 Runs were second in history

59 Home Runs were second in history (until Maris' 61)

457 Total Bases-first in history

.846 Slugging Average-second in history only to Babe's .847 in 1920!

10.9% Home Runs-third best ever. ('20, '27 Ruth)

119 Extra base hits-**first best** ever

171 RBIs-**personal best**

1.12 Runs batted in per game-second personal best (1.14 in 1929)

204 Hits-personal second best after 205 in 1923

144 Base on balls-tied third personal best

44 Doubles-second personal best, 45 in 1923

16 Triples-**personal best**

81 Strike-outs vs 89 in 1927

.378 Average-**ties personal best** in 1924

Pitching record of 2-0 in 1921!

American distortion of truth is evident. We seem to always be looking for the quick and easy labeled solution. Clearly 1921 was Babe's finest year, with out any asterisk! If only he didn't connect on September 30, 1927, the American mind would not have been so belittled. But only the great Bambino and Roger could not be stopped!

CHAPTER 14-4

It has been five pennant races since Peter M. Seitz turned the market around. So far the owners have taken a real beating.

To date there have been only four successful free agents. Only these elite have produced by being the catalyst of world championship stature!

First was Catfish, who was a breach of contract free agent, by the neglect of C.O. Finley. He is the last Yankee pitcher to win a World Series game. He brought the class it takes, to play all out even when being injured, just as Mickey did. When healthy and pitching to Munson, it was like a slice of baseball euphoria.

Of course there is Reggie, who rose to the occasion in Yankee fashion, during those famous Octobers. The Dodgers were blue and Reggie was enshrined.

Then there was Goose, who in his first year won all the marbles. Just to dispose of Yaz to clinch, in the *Greatest Playoff game,* was <u>well</u> worth the price.

Last year Mr. Rose did for the Phillies, what was hoped for but denied, for so long. The Phillies won by refusing to be defeated!

Well, tough luck for Cowboy Gene, and Brad C.!

By George...that's a .750 percentage for 5 years. Not too shabby!

Although the Yankees were <u>only</u> batting .750 at this point in time, the success of free agency was not lost. I had still been reading every box score or every selected player's box score. Rose was one that I had read and studied, nearly every game of his career. I can remember missing only two days until very late in his career. About 11-12 years before he broke Cobb's 4191 record, I told my father that he was in fact going to break this "unbreakable" record. Of course the response was "you cannot tell!" (i.e. "we'll see!") I insisted that nothing would hold him back. My friend Rick Karchefsky always did believe me. The point is that I loved the intensity that Rose played with, even if he has been said to be doing it for his own glorification, mentioned by Jim "Kitty" Kaat, the great baseball pitcher of twenty-five years. Besides, the Philadelphia victory made my great friend Dick Gilligan so happy. He knows that the '76ers cannot beat the Celtics!

CHAPTER 14-5

<u>A Winning Force</u>
<u>1983</u>

Reggie intimidates his world into a winning position. A strange psyche or not, he must be compared to Williams and Namath.

You see, if you hate Reggie Jackson you shouldn't even say a word. This is a corollary of Leary's double re-enforcement theory, but in the negative phase. If you don't like me because of my big mouth, and you tell me, then I'm going to beat you.

Reggie needs people. How else would one be able to sell from the negative point of view? It's an attitude not really of arrogance, but yet one of survival. In this world of dissension, building a force is easy.

Billy Martin was man enough to mitigate Reggie's great force and mellow it for years. No one, by any stroke of the imagination drove Reggie further than the Billy-George combo. Sometimes, or nearly always, results would be delayed, which emphasizes the lost degree of effectiveness of communication.

Don't forget the Yankees have not gone all the way for years now, of course it was Catfish's last win in the Series and the Captain was catching.

CHAPTER 14-6

Long Live Roger, Herb and "Sudden Sam"
4-2-87

With the fast-ball nearly of Koufax and in the fast lane of 1987, we finally fully understand the meaning of an asterisk. Dwight, Dr. K. Gooden, boy Phenom just exited his dream, and entered the "has beens", at twenty-two or so.

Commissioner Kuhn just had to denote Roger's record because of a few more games, BUT ALSO LESS THAN TEN MORE PLATE APPEARANCES THAN BABE!!

Dr. K., broke both Sam McDowell's one year record for the highest average of strikeouts, per game, and Herb Score's three year record.

In 1984 Doc Gooden set the record for Ks per game,

for a season. His average was 11.39. He also set the mark of 744 Ks in his first three years. A large asterisk should read by Dwight's records, denoting: *** This player has admitted to using illegal drugs and tested positively.**

Dr. K has just become "Doctor Loser" in the World Series of Life

PS. 1995

Thanks to my friends Joe T. and "Brother Wease" from WCMF, Rochester, N.Y. I have recently been reminded that Doc Ellis once pitched a no-hitter for the Pirates. During that game, he was allegedly or admitted that, he was "tripping on acid"! That game was played as the first game of a double-header, in San Diego, on June 12th, 1970. I wonder what he did in the clubhouse between games to celebrate!

THE DOCTORS HAVE THE <u>WRONG</u> PRESCRIPTION

THROW THE BUMS OUT FOREVER!

CHAPTER 14-7

<u>The Flower That Will Not Wilt!</u>

Swat...swat...swat... No that's not the sound of batting practice but the incredible Pete Rose with yet another immediate personal goal, and on the way to the TOP. At 40+ he senses a split season and an easy batting title. Easy the sense that it won't be the typical grind, that is not suited for big boys of 40.

The most amazing thing about the great Rose is his extreme concentration, conditioned reflex, and level of abstraction between the lines. Even when he was going through a traumatic divorce, he won a batting title and World Series! How can one worry about his son and daughter in the dugout, and perform like that on the field? He defies all odds. Nobody has "seen the seams" more often.

Some call it a nose for the ball. I call it a clear flowing channeled semantic reaction. Rose's psyche for short, was at a high against the Red Sox in the Series. Fisk tried to psyche out the master. But the next day it was Rose who scored the winner and in the ninth, with one out and miles to go, it was Rose who was playing 3rd base, when a pop-up went over his head. Pete called off the whole stadium, whether the ball was his or not. Everyone knew that he would **never** miss it.

The last out in the Pittsburgh series was anticlimactic, although it was nip and tuck all the way. But with one out in the ninth, the ball popped out of the catcher's glove, and like a magnetic force someone grabbed the ball out of mid-air, for out number two. Everyone knew it had to be Rose again.

Many people who were not believers before, had better watch out now. I think Ty just rolled over.

CHAPTER 14-8

The "Pine Tar" Kid Fights Back
written 10-3-90

What George Brett did last night was etch his name in stone. This time the fight was of different proportions. He did not rant and rave as he did when his homer off Goose Gossage, was apparently taken away. Brett was restrained there, but not in this personal battle.

At thirty-seven years old, he was hitting just .240, at the All-Star game! Then George started to wave his magic stick and proceeded to beat out today's best player in the game, Rickey Henderson, for high average! This feat was truly phenomenal.

The press hardly understood the accomplishment of winning a batting championship in three decades and ten years apart at his age. Brett's astounding comeback was as basic as driving through the ball with good work habits, especially keeping his front shoulder closed longer. He was extremely smart to let Rickey catch up for a bit at the end, because today he ensured a first-ballot selection.

A chance of a lifetime, and Brett seized the moment. Both his home run off the "Goose" was restored and so was his batting crown. If I were George, I would play just one more year, hit .301 and retire. I would also then purchase a New York State road map, in the next five years.

PS George actually isn't that bad of a name for a ballplayer. There was once a George Ruth and a George Seaver that played a little.

CHAPTER 14-9

The Gloomiest Day

I was standing out in front of my grammar school (Hosea Rogers) just seconds after the final bell rang! I took the chance of running down the hall in order to get out as fast as I could. I was not enough of a risk-taker to listen to the World Series in school because that was strictly against the rules. The year was 1960, the month was October, and this was game seven.

My friendly transistor radio was jammed in to my ear. I had put a new battery in just that morning for this occasion. I remembered to purchase one just the week before the Series and save it. I still had a dollar or two saved up from cutting lawns. I purposely purchased this, my first transistor radio, with the Series in mind. It set me back about $5.50! Roger had informed me of the best one to buy. Now I was not playing attention to anyone.

I was confident that the Yankees would "do it" again because they were the Yankees and although the Series was tied at three games each, they had been mashing the ball and far out-slugging the Pirates. They had romped in their three wins 16-3, 10-0, 12-0! (The Yankees did also set a record by collecting an amazing 91 hits in that Series!) However, I was aware of how awful it felt to lose, no thanks to Lew Burdette in 1957. Thank God we came back after being down 3-1 in 1958.

It was getting late in the game and finally I was squeezing out each mighty important out. The Yankees were up 7-4 at the beginning of the inning but the Pirates opened with a single by Gino Cimoli. I started to pray for a ground ball. Suddenly the announcer says "Virdon hits a ground ball to short" YES that's it we've got it! Suddenly the ball took a bad hop and hit Kubek in the throat. For a second I wasn't sure if Tony still made the play or not, but I was still hoping. A split second later it's clarified that Kubek was down and there was no play. At THAT moment I had the feeling of impending doom! I still tried to believe that that play was an isolated incidence and would not turn the tide, but already at the age of eleven and one-half, I was aware of plays of fate. Kubek had to be hospitalized. Soon it was 7-5 with runners at second and third, one out. I'm now holding my breath. Finally there was a fly to right with no advance, WHEW! Then Clemente hit one in the infield, I was again praying for a play, but the weak chopper went for a hit! A run scored and I was shuddering. Next Hal Smith got up and connected off reliever Jim Coates. I was absolutely stunned! The Pirates were now leading 9-7.

I kept on saying to myself, "we can come back because we are the Yankees and we never give up!" If only Mickey would get up this inning! The Yankees started a rally and Mickey did get up, with one out and runners at first and third. As usual he delivered, by singling in a run in the ultimate clutch situation. Mickey was now on first and Yogi smashed a grounder to the Pirates first baseman Rocky Nelson. Nelson stepped on the bag and then Mickey again pulled the ultimate "Mick Sharp" play by diving back into first under Nelson's tag! The tying run scored on the play! The Yankees ended their half in a tie. Of course, Mazeroski then led off the bottom of the ninth and Ralph Terry suddenly became eternal friends with Ralph Branca! I was ready to "ralph"!

I was so shaken that my knees were weak! I had tears in my eyes and could not believe that damn transitor radio. Maybe there had been a mistake! I was so choked up that I really could not breathe too well. I listened closer and the announcer then verified the outcome of the game. My throat was full of phlegm, my windpipe felt clogged and I felt light-headed. I wasn't sure if I could walk home, which was only seven or eight minutes! I talked myself into "getting it together" enough to leave. I suddenly was struck with a new fear. I couldn't bear the thought of running into one of those jerky Yankee haters. **That** would be the ultimate humiliation.

Little did I know that Mickey, who had a great Series,(.400, 10 hits, 11 RBI) was crying at the same time that I was! He was in the trainer's room and when he finally stopped bawling, he asked about how Tony was doing?

It has been thirty-five years now and I'm still not quite over that one yet, the same way that Yogi is today still pissed that he is positive that he had Jackie Robinson tagged out on his steal of home plate, and was called safe! I had experienced the agony of defeat before in 1955 and remember first hand when Yogi hit that fly ball into the left-field corner, when the Yankees had to make their move (down 2-0 in the sixth). I was quite sure that it would fall in there and tie the score and suddenly Sandy Amoros slid and speared the ball. What a let down! I can also remember 1957 and Spahn, but mainly Burdette. At least that made Mark real happy. However this one was different and more devastating because the Yankees were statistically creaming the Pirates.

It was there and then, that I learned the value of baseball statistics. Now when some Madison Avenue announcer tells me that Ozzie Smith hasn't hit a homer in nine zillion years, especially against this pitcher, especially in the World Series, I just turn to Adam and say "here it goes!" The next pitch ... IT DID! That one, quite frankly, was the easiest one to predict. Anyway, I didn't know any true Pirate fans in 1960, just Yankee haters, and really couldn't give a damn!

They say that within every tragedy or adverse event, and this was a tragedy, that there is somewhere a silver lining. All you have to do is look hard enough, but sometimes it is not apparent right away. More than thirty years had passed and I now have met some great friends that grew up in Pittsburgh. One being Mike Miller, who was a captain in the Air Force when serving our great country. Mike always wanted to "be" Roberto. I have had many discussions about "strata" of the players and "real" superstars of that era! I'm not sure that Mike agrees to this day, which shows you what a good man he is!

Jack Senay, who always wanted to "be" Ralph Kiner,

is a most wonderful human being. He knows exactly who he is and has exact and well defined priorities. He is the ultimate family man. He is extremely creative and idea centered when it comes to our work. I have had the delight of working with Jack and having him be my mentor, for the last few years! By the way, when I was out on the sidewalk crying he was riding the streetcar home from Prep School, through downtown Pittsburgh, in an instant TICKER TAPE PARADE!

Everyone of the baby-boomer generation, can tell you precisely where they were and what they were doing, when our lives were turned around, by the shooting of President Kennedy. I can remember that I was in Biology class, Mr. Frank Sacco, tenth grade, but all the details are not vivid. I can much better remember that shot that was fired, the 13th day of October, 1960!

Bobby Kennedy profoundly reminded us that "time heals all wounds." This year (1995) the Yankees have just blown the first "Wild Card" Series, by playing well but losing three in a row! They just didn't have the killer instinct needed, a bit like in 1976, before Munson selected his help. (Reggie). I must be maturing a little because I actually got a few hours of sleep following this years' loss, although I was not thinking about 1960!

CHAPTER 14-10

The Greatest Home Run was "Meant To Be"!

If you believe no other story in this book, albeit they are all exact accounts of my recollection, please believe this one.

It was a Wednesday night, in May of 1963. That was the first night that I had ever gone anywhere with Garry Hurwitz, and without Mark. We went to the JYMA of Rochester, New York to play basketball. Garry was almost two years older, but only one grade ahead of me, since I had started grammar school at the age of four. Mark was in my class. We took the city bus up and back to the gym.

The night was balmy, almost like that first perfect night

in June. Garry and I had no trouble bonding further and had a good time playing basketball. When we exited the bus, Garry was on the higher step just behind me. Suddenly he "flicked" my ear (as we were hitting the sidewalk), which was a common practice during that stage of our lives! Soon he attempted to do it again and again and I deflected his hand on both new attempts. I wouldn't put up with his nonsense and started to sprint ahead, a few yards or so, up the two blocks that we had to go.

At this point of my life I was just getting out of my husky Yogi-like stage and for the first time was gaining some speed. Garry, on the other hand, always had a much slimmer build, 5'10" or so and 145 pounds or less, and he was much faster. Garry was now turning on the speed to catch me, but I was determined not to let him "flick" my ear again because that hurt, but more importantly, ear flicks were psychologically demeaning. No **"man"** would take that without a battle. I soon heard his feet, just one-half of a stride behind me. He reached out and grazed my shoulder, and I once again further accelerated ahead. Garry also turned on the speed and I again further accelerated ahead. Garry also turned on the speed and again nearly had me in his grasp, and yet again, I turned up the speed, as if I was in a "run-down," with two outs in the bottom of the ninth.

We both were laughing and really beginning to enjoy this strange camaraderie! Every time he sped up, I continued to sprint faster than I had ever sprinted before in my life! This exercise continued nearly all the way to his yard, before he gave up! We were in high spirits and laughing loudly upon entering the far end of his circular driveway. The usual 8 to 10 minute walk most certainly took us well under one-half that time. It was probably

128

that event, that started our mutual admiration of sporting determination and a closer friendship.

Suddenly Mark yelled out of his upstairs bedroom window, where only the screen was down, because of the fine weather. "Bob, if you hurry you can hear Mickey's at bat!" I was taken by surprise to hear Mark's voice. Obviously he wasn't in my thoughts those past few moments. I quickly yelled "WHAT?" Mark yelled "HURRY MICKEY'S UP. IF YOU PEEL YOU CAN CATCH HIM!"

I took off like a shot, thank God that I was all warmed up! My first thought was that my estimated arrival time would be eight to ten seconds to get to the front door of my house (I wouldn't settle for twelve) and another five or so until my radio was on in my room! Suddenly I had the clearest premonition of my baseball life!!! **"If Mickey is batting left-handed, he is going to hit one."** It was so clear that I sort of even verbalized it. That thought was weird because although Mickey hit many a "Ruthian" shot lefty, I lived to see him swing from the right side, with that raw power like **NOBODY** else, had ever displayed! My father instantly saw me "tear in" and down the hall. Streaking past, I simply yelled "MICKEY'S UP." He understood.

My radio was on in a flash and of course it was left on the Yankee station. The first words or sounds that I then heard were **"THE RIGHT HANDER IS RUBBING UP THE BALL!"** I cringed, smiled, and said "oh my God, what amazement that the announcer would even say that, and at this exact moment in my life!" Most often they would say "the pitcher or call him by his last name, is rubbing up the ball." That righty was Bill Fischer of the Kansas City A's!

Next came the words that I have the clearest recollection of in my life, besides my father's 1954 lecture! (Actually that is debatable because of Vic Power!)...**"MANTLE SWINGS AND THAT BALL IS GONE AND STILL RISING! I THINK IT IS OUT OF YANKEE STADIUM!...OH MY GOD, IT HIT THE FACADE, WITH A THUD JUST BELOW THE TOP OF THE FACADE!"**

I sat on my bed with tears of awe. It was then explained that because of how hard the ball was hit, and how it was still rising at a tremendous rate, that if the Stadium was built just a foot or two deeper, that the ball would have gained a few more inches in height, and been out of the Stadium, for the first time in history. It was nearly 400 feet away, nearly 120 feet high, and hit the facade with a loud audible thud! I was literally numb. After a few minutes of listening to the cheers, I suddenly got a different feeling. I was pissed that it didn't go out. I had been aware of that possibility because that was now the second time that Mickey had hit the facade! Mark and I had often debated if it was even humanly possible to hit a ball out of Yankee Stadium, and my conclusion was always that *only* Mickey could do it... What a chain of events, what a night!, May 22, 1963!

For the next thirty two years I never understood why that ball didn't leave Yankee Stadium. I now understand that those "precious" few inches were all that separated Mickey from being immortal! Maybe if that ball had left the premises, Mickey and Whitey would have celebrated too much and gotten into a career-ending accident. Or maybe Mickey was just supposed to keep trying (to do it right!) for five more years. Anyway, thank you Mickey, thank you GOD, or is that redundant?

CHAPTER 14-11

<u>Little League, Yesterday and Today</u>

Most children are thrilled to finally get the chance to play in an organized baseball league. That is your start, with the ultimate progression of playing in high school, college, and to play for the New York Yankees. Then you can "be" Mickey or Yogi! At nine, I was as anxious as anyone alive. The only problem was that you then had to be ten to sign up in Irondequoit, my home town. Without hesitation my father took me to a town about twenty-five minutes away (Charlotte). They allowed nine-year-olds to play in their program. I was so happy!

During the first "on field" check-in and organization meeting, I was standing with a group of ten kids or so. My father was standing with the group. Soon the league director asked him his name and asked if he would watch the kids <u>for a moment?</u> A few minutes later the director came back and said , "Bernie take *your* team to the other end of the field to assemble and practice!"

Little League got lucky that time, and so did I. He taught me how to play baseball, how to coach and manage a baseball team, children, parents, administrators, and people in general, and all with class and dignity. Baseball was that wonderful vehicle that forever kept me occupied and taught me about life!

That was the year that I began to learn the art of catching, and little did I know then, the art of umpiring, as they were hanging over your shoulder. Actually I was learning the whole game, each position and every situation, because the whole game is in front of you and you are involved on every pitch. What a gift from heaven!

Little League was a bit political back then also. For instance, "Catfish" Eggert was never once on my team until Pony League or higher, because there was always a deal, or an arrangement for his services. That was okay because I still caught a million pitches for him, and found that I could hit him. I remember that I was a little scared inside because he was *good*, but I never, ever admitted that or showed that side to Paul. I just walked around like it was no big deal. I guess those certain days I wanted to `be' Reggie!

Little League was fun and positive because even then (ten years and up) you realized that some teams were loaded with talent, but that was a small portion of our learning and playing time. The main emphasis of playing baseball was during our sandlot games and Little League was in essence "just a show" for the parents. Unfortunately today it is most likely the only show.

I do wish today's parents would better understand that point. Today children play a few hours here and there and rarely practice outside of organized ball. Parents seem to go ballistic about Johnny not playing a certain position, not enough innings, batting in a certain position, the fields, the umpiring, the uniforms, the rules and a whole myriad of issues, not to mention, **winning at all costs.** The vast majority of times the coaches are fair, but the parents can only see "truth" for their own child and do not see or do not want to see the big picture. Too often they are the same parents who do not get involved except on mandatory snack bringing day. This hurts me because our children suffer the consequences.

On the other hand, you can run into some of the nicest people in the world too. Some years ago, during an initial parent meting of the season a parent asked me the most basic and legitimate question that was ever asked. "What gives you the qualifications to coach my son?" I was flabbergasted and laughed! At that time I had played, coached, managed, administrated, umpired and lived baseball for a lifetime. But the point of the matter is that that parent understood the vulnerability of the Little League credentialing process. Rick Aab and his wife Jackie have become our lifelong friends, starting with that question. Rick helped me coach along with Dick Reese, whose wife Karen has done a fantastic job being the secretary of the Board of Directors of Pittsford Little League, for at least five years. If you are looking for nicer people in this world, you will never find them.

Richard T. Aab is a class gentleman. He is a self-made man and the Chairman of ACC Corp., which he has toiled at for years, as president and CEO. Rick built his business up from scratch to where it is today. He went to

133

college on a soccer scholarship, has won a club championship in golf and shot five consecutive rounds in the 70's this year, while he was traveling 70-90 hours a week!

His real love is baseball. He tells his employees to make sure that they manage their schedules so they can do their work and be at the children's games. He often runs through airports and shows up on time for the first pitch. The line-ups that he makes out are great. Rick Aab has done more good for people than anyone that I have ever met in my life.

Just last week Jill and I went out to dinner with Rick and Jackie. The four of us arrived a few minutes late for our reservations because we were engrossed in a rerun of *The Twilight Zone!* The evening had already started out very nicely. After ordering dinner I started talking to Rick, about playing baseball as a child. Soon we discussed "Homerun Ball" and I asked him who he wanted to "be?" Rick looked at me PRECISELY like I looked at him years earlier, (with his first question) a bit insulted, laughed and said, **"WHAT, ARE YOU KIDDING ME?!!!!"**. I had never actually asked him that question before. It was then that I told him of this book.

I do not have a quick and "sure fire" answer to solve all the problems of today's Little Leagues. We do need more parent involvement and "Rick Aabs" as bosses to make this happen. Most importantly we need to remember that this is our children's sandlot time.

Everyone needs great friends to pull them through in crunch time. Rick, Jackie, Dick, Karen and Jill help me keep my perspective with the issues of Little League. Jill has a *most* wonderful friend in Teresa Nicosia and in Denise Kendricks at her school. They are both fantastic human beings and great Yankee fans! Thanks to all. Little

League has been great to me. I hope and pray that it is great for our children.

CHAPTER 15

<u>Returning the Favor, Ala Carte</u>
<u>1992</u>

The tingling up my spine, with that first view of Yankee Stadium, has been with me for nearly thirty years. Finally it was time to return the favor that my father bestowed upon me.

Robert Kowal DDS is my doubles partner in racquetball, a super athlete and, just like his best friend Joe Klein, the *mensch* of all *mensches*. Robbie has never seen me play ball other than a little coaching of his son Brian, but he has seen me play some third-base on the racquetball court. He has a keen eye for talent, and hates to lose about as much as I do. He is also a great Yankee fan. He graduated from Dental School at NYU a few years back.

Robbie's son Brian is also friends with my son Adam. With everyone being friends and Yankee fans, the stage was now set for our big trip.

It was an easy decision to take the boys to the "Big Apple". The schedule was perfect because the Yankees were at home and playing a Sunday matinee followed by a Monday evening game at Shea. We had no desire to go to Yankee Stadium at night. It is inevitable that George will soon "book out". We left Rochester on Saturday after Robbie's patients were taken care of, about 4 p.m. Adam had been home from camp just 23 hours and already we were running to baseball! Life is great and so is Jill.

Before we went to see the Yankees play Boston we stopped into a *few* places to eat. Robbie took us immediately to "Little Italy" and to the delectable Anthony's. We knocked off seven loaves of bread just waiting for our dinner. We proceeded or rather rolled out the door and went next door for dessert at the famous La Farara's Bakery. The apple pie ala mode was fantastic. I really never have had better in my life, and the portions were enormous. Before leaving Robbie ordered a couple of cannoli for us to try! We went back to our hotel in Flushing at midnight and Robbie asked if we were hungry. Adam and I politely refused, laughed and went to bed. We needed our rest for the big day.

Sunday morning we met in the lobby to make plans for the day. I forgot my newspaper upstairs and informed Robbie that I was going to run up to get it. Robbie said that he and the kids would be in the small hotel dining area. I was not hungry and neither were the boys. Robbie had a quick bowl of cereal by the time I had returned.

They say that the most important meal of the day is

breakfast and Robbie had a special place to take us for our real breakfast. We piled into the car. Robbie was now driving because, although I was passing almost every taxi, we weren't going fast enough. I buckled my seat belt. Robbie took us to Ratner's on the lower east side because they have fantastic blintzes, but it was a minor Jewish holiday and they were closed. Robbie, of course, knew that the famous deli Katz's was just up the block. We entered Katz's at ten o'clock in the morning, and Adam ordered breakfast first. "I'll have the chicken noodle soup please."

Robbie blurted out, "Chicken noodle soup?" as if Adam were nuts. I quickly looked at the chef mixing up the soup and it truly looked delicious. I said that I would have the same. Robbie and I had been talking about "going light" and just having pancakes. Robbie was not sure that this was really happening. Brian looked at that huge bowl of soup, overflowing with noodles, with a side order of huge pieces of fresh rye bread and butter. Brian said "It looks scrumptious.. I'll have the same!"

Robbie ordered pancakes and eggs and exclaimed "You're all nuts".

We were all eating and talking about a kid named Sam Militello, who was making his major league debut today, for the Yankees. We were aware of the awesome trust put in this young man, because we *are* playing the Red Sox. Suddenly Robbie got up and ordered "a side" of soup declaring "It does look good." He returned with the same size bowl as we had. Robbie polished off his pancakes, eggs and soup. After enjoying a nourishing breakfast and the Yankee-like conversation, we left and Robbie coerced us to trot back down to Ratner's, thinking that they may now have opened, because they have great pastries and desserts. Ratner's was still closed.

We were now on the way to Yankee Stadium, and Robbie made a comment about how good the hot dogs will be at Yankee Stadium. Adam, Brian and I *plotzed*.

The boys and I were a bit scared walking from the parking lot. It was a few blocks away from the Stadium, but I did not have to use the small *Mace* canister, that I have had for years, because of jogging. My finger was on the trigger just in case. Robbie, on the other hand, slipped away to the other side of the street. He was already in the process of upgrading our tickets through a street scalper.

Finally we entered Yankee Stadium and the boys were awe stricken. Adam said that he felt a chill going up his spine. Brian's eyes were glassy and as big as saucers. Robbie had an extremely satisfying look of a very proud father on his face, or else he had just passed gas from breakfast.

I quickly got instructions on how to get to the entrance of Monument Park. This site sits beyond the left-field fence, where the monuments of Ruth, Huggins and Gehrig now reside. The man said that we had better hurry because they close one hour before the game, and there was usually a line to get in. Adam and I started peeling and weaving through, the already large crowd. As luck would have it, we were at the farthest point away from our destination. Adam and I were very adept at these maneuvers due to experiencing Buffalo Bills games, with rowdy crowds and lack of bathrooms.

We were now losing Brian and Robbie with still a long way to go. Robbie, who was still fighting break-fast, signaled us to slow down. We stopped and quickly agreed that we would meet him and Brian in the Park.

Time was now of the essence, because Adam knew that my lifelong dream has been to someday return the favor. Adam and I just made it in under the wire. We were having a heavenly "baseball" father and son time. Besides the monuments, there are remembrances of Jake Ruppert, Mickey, Joe D, Yogi, Thurman, Roger, Billy Martin, Whitey and so many more. Suddenly Adam had a notion that maybe Robbie didn't make it because he had a heart attack! I did that fatherly "guy" thing and assured Adam that Robbie was okay, and that we are extraordinary at getting through crowds. I was praying inside for Robbie.

After this euphoric start, we headed back to our seats. Thank God Robbie and Brian were sitting calmly and enjoying the scenery and warm-up drills. Robbie announces that they hadn't felt like running way over there, so they stopped for a hot dog. We were in a great mood because the Yankees were easily handling Boston. Militello pitched a great game, holding Boston to one hit in seven innings. Steve Farr relieved and also allowed no hits. Donzie went 1-3 and drove in a RBI. We romped 6-0! Adam and Brian were now 1 for 1 at the Stadium. The mission was complete.

We returned to the hotel elated with the outcome of the game, and Robbie started a discussion of dinner options. The bell captain then told Robbie that right out the door is an excellent Asian Cuisine restaurant that would also make anything the boys wanted. They do like chicken. This man walked us over to the restaurant, called the owner his friend out from the back and told him to take good care of us. We started with appetizers that were on the house. That was followed by a copious amount of chicken, with various side dishes. Robbie and the boys had dessert.

Monday morning we ate breakfast at the hotel in the dining area. We were concerned about parking in Manhattan so we split the cab fare going to downtown. The Met's game wasn't until that evening. Minutes after we got out of the taxi, Robbie said "How about some fresh bagels?" We bought four, with cream cheese on the side, and were eating them as we walked. Just a few minutes later, we passed a street vendor selling fresh squeezed orange juice and Robbie *had* to have some. The rest of us declined. Brian now looked shell-shocked at the intake of food, by his Dad! Robbie paid $2.25 for about 3 to 4 ounces of juice but said it was delicious. He had trouble handling the juice, the rest of the bagel and the left over cream cheese and asked me to hold his bagel for a minute. After Robbie savored the juice, he latched onto the bagel as we headed up 51st Street. Two blocks later, Robbie saw and smelled an appealing donut shop. He insisted that we have a few. We bought four and divvied them up.

We had a tremendous time walking through the tour of Manhattan. Soon after FOA Schwartz Toys, we went into The Sharper Image. After browsing for a few moments Robbie saw a demonstration model of a digital scale. Out of the clear blue he looked at me and said, "I bet you that I weigh more than you do now." Robbie had just gotten down to about 165 pounds on a bet with Joe. I typically hold between 175 and 180 pounds. I was *positive* that I still had him shaded after the enormous proportions that we had just consumed. Robbie insisted that we bet a quarter. I insisted that he shouldn't bet me. Robbie then demanded that we bet. He hopped on the scale and registered 181. I hopped on and registered 182! Robbie abruptly flipped me a quarter and stormed out of the store! He has never bet me on anything since.

Next we went to Mickey Mantle's restaurant and took the full tour, including the articles in the bathroom. We decided not to eat lunch there because this time I had a better choice. We went to the New York City Deli. We sat down and Robbie got an explanation of just how large the sandwiches are. Brian is not a real large boy at twelve and neither is Adam. The waitress said that they also have a half of sandwich on the menu, but Robbie decided that we should "go for broke." Adam and I both ordered full-size turkey sandwiches, Brian and Robbie ordered full-size pastrami and roast beef sandwiches. While waiting, we were knocking off all the dill pickles and dill tomatoes that we could handle. Soon the sandwiches arrived and they were nearly ten inches high! Never in my life have I ever put that much turkey on my plate, even at Thanksgiving! Robbie ordered Brian to start eating. It was so good that I finished the entire sandwich. Adam ate more than I had ever seen him put away, a little over one-half. Brian followed his father's orders, eating nearly one-half. Robbie finished his roast beef sandwich and then devoured the other half of Brian's pastrami sandwich! We were all ready to leave and Robbie said, "How about getting a *knish?*" He insisted that we'll just try a little piece. He called the waitress over and ordered a potato *knish*. The *knish* arrived in a few minutes and it was larger than a personal pan pizza, and about six times heavier. Robbie made sure that we all try it. It was fantastic. Robbie ate about two-thirds; we split the rest! On the way out Robbie whispered in my ear, "This place can kill you!"

"So have the other nineteen places that we just stopped at," I responded.

142

We got back to the hotel about 3 o'clock, which was just time enough to freshen up and relax for a bit. Robbie announced that we'd eat dinner at the game!

Then he had another good idea. He really wants to quickly stop back on the Lower East Side, because he thought that I should buy the leather jacket that I had tried on yesterday. Off we go to the wheel and deal. We parked in the exact same block as yesterday. The jacket started at three hundred yesterday and after two different attempts with the store owner, we were down to two hundred. I had offered $100 cash but did not pull out the cash because the owner had laughed. Robbie and I decided that I should offer $150 maximum today. I started by waving six twenties in front of the man. He quickly responded that the leather jacket is mine for $140. Robbie was thrilled for me. Jill even liked it when we got home. As we were walking towards the car, Robbie says that he was going to run down one block to Ratner's! To Ratner's we went and Robbie bought a few pastries for us to try!

We left for the game, with the jacket buried in the trunk, so that we would still be in time to see all of batting practice. We went in through the turnstile and <u>before</u> we took our seats, Robbie polished off a hot dog!...I swear that this is the truth. We had front row box seats just as we upgraded for in Yankee Stadium. But people at Shea were constantly walking in front of us and it was very disturbing. We now wished that there was some way to buy lower box seats so we wouldn't be interrupted. At Yankee Stadium there were more exit ramps and therefore fewer people passing in front of us, disturbing our concentration. Robbie is a great father and I can see he's quite disturbed at messing up the kids' day. He bought cokes and peanuts for the boys.

We conferred about the seating and I informed him that I didn't have the foggiest notion how to pay off an usher. Maybe it wouldn't be so bad once the game started. The game began and the distractions weren't much better. After the first inning, Robbie approached the head usher of that section, and pleaded our case about "returning the dream" to our children. Robbie made eye contact or approached him after each half inning, three more times. Robbie then smiled and reported that we would be "taken care of" soon.

After the third inning the usher subtly nods for us to come down the ramp, out of sight. Robbie slipped him a twenty. The usher ordered the kids to take off their hats, put them under their arms and swiftly follow him. He marched the four of us down about thirty rows or so. There were four unused corporate box seats! Brian and Adam swiftly took the two front row seats, with their noses literally out on the playing field, right next to Eddie Murray, who was playing first base! (Correct!). Robbie and I sat directly behind our sons. "How's this?" Robbie asked, followed by, "How about a hot-dog and a beer?"

This day was meant to be. The game lasted sixteen innings. In that time Robbie ordered an array of food from the vendors. They also went once to the concession stand for pizza. About the thirteenth inning the crowd started to dwindle. Robbie sprawled out a bit which gave him a better look at the remaining vendors roaming around. He got excited upon seeing a cotton candy vendor. He promptly ordered one for each boy. Since Robbie hadn't had cotton candy for ages, he tried a little. I tried one bite and felt like I was going to barf! We negotiated about how long we would stay because it was now at least 1 a.m. We had to catch a flight at about 7 a.m. We agreed that we would leave after the 14th inning regardless of the status of the game.

We had a long walk to the car and I suggested that we might as well stay inside the Stadium, as we were walking out, and maybe we would still catch some action. Just before our exit Robbie spotted an ice cream vendor. The kids were "punch drunk" now because it was 1:40 a.m.. Adam hadn't had a decent night's sleep in the last three weeks!

The three of them were standing there eating ice-cream cones and watching the game. I then told Robbie that the only good pinch hitter that the Mets have left was Doc Gooden. We were walking through the parking lot when we heard some loud cheers. The Mets ended up losing 4-2 to the Pirates. Eddie Murray was hitless and Bonds managed two hits. Andy Van Slyke hit the ball on the button, nearly all eight times up but got only three hits. Doc Gooden pinch hit in the sixteenth, and went 1 for 1!

Back at the hotel, Robbie considered going back to our Asian restaurant. It was now past 2 o'clock when I finally talked him out of it.

We "slept fast" as the old expression goes. The morning went smoothly after waking up at 5 a.m. We had to hustle our rental car back. At the airport I got in line with all of the tickets so that we could confirm our seats and check our bags. We would have a ten to fifteen minute wait for our flight. Robbie slipped out for a quick breakfast!

Just a few weeks ago I met Robbie to play racquetball. "When in the hell is Steinbrenner going to get Cone, already?" I demanded. Robbie fully agreed to the urgency. The next morning's headlines read that the Yankees got both Cone and Sierra! The Yankees locked up the "Wild

Card" spot nearly two months later, on the last regular day of the season.

My daughter Lauren has been bothering me to take her to New York, especially to Yankee Stadium, because she likes baseball and loves to play softball. She has a dream of playing very competitive softball for years to come. Lauren works hard to maintain a high degree of physical conditioning. I think she would be better off going to New York with Jill and Robbie's wife and daughter, Janet and Rachel.

How can you not love Robbie Kowal? The whole world does.

CHAPTER 16

<u>Louie's Best Catch</u>

The art of collecting baseball cards and memorabilia has always intrigued me. I'm sure that this feeling was accentuated at Wallack's drug store in early May, 1958. By the 1963 season I was old enough to fully realize that the 1961 Yankees would probably never happen again. I intuitively started writing to the nine starters i.e. Bobby, Tony, Roger, Mickey, Yogi, Elston, Moose, Cletis and Whitey (and some other top stars, namely Aaron and Koufax) for their autographs. To each I sent a self-addressed stamped envelope including a neatly folded piece of paper, and a quick individualized note to ensure a positive outcome. The note was a creative way to beg my heroes for their signature.

To Mickey I wrote, "I'll be watching when you hit one off Sandy in the World Series." The Dodgers and Yankees were still months away from the end of the pennant race. Mickey did send me his autograph and I was "as high as kite" for weeks and years. I have since taught my son Adam of the same methodology. He begged Joe DiMaggio on the fact that Adam was born on Joe's 65th birthday and that he wanted to "be" Joe D.. Upon arrival of Joe's signature, Adam was thrown into the same euphoria. Autographs do not usually have the same monetary worth of cards, but I question which are really more valuable?

Lo and behold the Yankees and Dodgers both made it to the Series. Before the fourth game my cousin Stuart Nobel, now Stuart Allen, decided that he wanted to simulate a betting pool by innings. I thought for a minute and told him that I will take the Yankees in the seventh. He asked me why, and I responded that that is when Mickey will be up. Koufax was going to take the mound that day. We bet, and sure enough, when Mickey got up in the seventh inning he hit a home run, off Koufax! I netted one-third of the pot, which was 75 cents. Stuie was pissed and asked "how did you know?" You can also look this up, Stuart lives in the Tampa area. I did not have the gumption to tell cousin Stuie about the letter to Mickey. I guess during that period, I wanted to "be" Carnack!

Collecting has been and still is a great tradition in the Kravetz family. Louis Kravetz, my paternal grandfather, was an entomologist. He actually started collecting butterflies in the 1940's. One day upon one his many excursions he saw a man turning over rocks and examining the area. He quickly said to my grandmother Bessie "what

148

is he doing?" Soon Bessie investigated and reported that he was looking for beetles. Louie told Bessie "if I ever start doing that, I'll have my head examined!" Apparently that day grandpa Louie wanted to "be" Sigmund Freud! Soon after, he started to collect, organize, categorize, pin and mount in professional display cases, beetles.

For at least twenty five years, Louis passionately collected beetles from all over the world. By the early 1960's he had found and collected every specimen known in New York State. Often the family had heard about the tiger beetle which was "impossible to catch". When challenged about the probability of catching the tiger he would emphatically explain why it was impossible. "**You don't understand**, he would demand". Than he would put his two index fingers on his forehead like tentacles and become very animated. In his beautiful slight accent simulate the tiger's defense, "they just sit there and watch you until you get six or eight feet away and then if you make a move (exploding his fingers) and poof, they would fly away!"

In 1964 my grandparents went with my father and I on *the* New York City trip with my first look at the Yankees and the World's Fair. We stayed at my Uncle Sam's and Aunt Mildred Stickler's (Louie's sisters') apartment, on Shore Parkway, in Canarsie, N.Y. A morning or two after seeing the Yankees for the first time, my grandfather and I went to the Jamaica Bay beach, where tiger beetles hang out, near the water. Louie always carried his beetle bottles (a small test tube like glass container with a removable cork in the end) in his pocket. That day, he also brought his precious butterfly net. I was now fifteen and as cocky as you would expect any fifteen year old kid to be. Besides I had just seen Mickey get up with the bases loaded, at Yankee Stadium, and rope a line drive. I promptly told my grandfather "I'm going to catch a tiger beetle for you Zadie." I was as brash as Joe Willie was soon to be on his prediction of winning the Super Bowl with the Jets, five years later. He promptly responded, "**You can't**!" We were soon on the beach and Louie saw a tiger and *just* as he says, poof it was gone. This happened a few more times exactly the same way, and he again emphatically said, "**See, you cannot catch them**". For a moment I was discouraged but I was still only fifteen years old. I had never seen Mickey or Yogi give up.

I begged my grandfather for the net. He was very reluctant to hand me one of his most precious possessions. Soon I insisted that I would not damage the net. Finally he agreed. I tried two or three times to swoop the tiger with no success and he repeated, "**see, you cannot do it**" To me that had the exact impact as Koufax after a loss! I begged for more chances and then I had an idea. I started to walk slowly away from the "tiger" and then uncoiled, lunged, stretched my reach to the max and swooped at the "tiger". The net had landed adjacent to the tiger before he flew off! My grandfather's eyes were popping out his skull. He demanded that I give him the net and now I was reluctant to give the net to him! One more time, creep away, creep, creep, uncoil, spring, lunge...zap. I landed in the sand and I swore that I had one! We quickly looked and see our prize under the net! Louie immediately put a ton of pressure around the rim and reached for his bottle. I told my grandfather that I would make the exchange into the bottle. He had been waiting for this dream longer than I had been waiting to see Mickey at the Stadium! He smiled and nudged me back. VERY methodically he squeezed the "tiger" into the bottle and we were at least as "high" as I had been upon entering the down ramp of Yankee Stadium!

Suddenly Louie said, "give me that net!" He tried about five times in vain to net his prey. I told him to explode! Then he uncoiled like Ruth did, in his last great game at Pittsburgh, hitting three home runs and the last one cleared the ball park! Louie was determined and suddenly looked like he is seventeen, for a split second, although he was at least sixty six. **Zap...Louis Kravetz just caught the `tiger' on his own!** For the first time in my life I realized what it meant to truly be elated for someone else.

After my grandfather passed away, Jill and I housed his collection for a number of years. We knew that the collection would just deteriorate if it wasn't properly taken care of. Just before a scheduled trip to Washington, our neighbor Mary Beth Feindt took high quality pictures of each of the twenty one and one-half cases. The specimens were meticulously mounted and labeled. Two tiny cards were also included. One card was for the genus and species, the other stated who found it, where it was found and the date. All cards were hand printed by Louis. Jill and I met with the chief curator of the Division of Entomology at the Smithsonian Institute.

Upon breaking the news to the family, it was decided that we should keep the collection in Rochester, N.Y. Soon thereafter we met with the curators of the Rochester Museum and Science Center. Bob Cooper informed me that "the collection was the most organized collection that he had ever seen in his life!" Soon the Rochester Museum and Science Center rebuilt their museum, with the Louis Kravetz collection being the cornerstone exhibit. Somewhere in those 5,234 specimens are the "tigers", one reading, caught by Louis Kravetz, Canarsie, N.Y., 1964!

Collecting does still run in the family. Lee Johnson is my brother-in-law and a class guy. If it weren't for the fact that he grew up rooting for the Brooklyn Dodgers, we could be blood brothers. Lee is five years older than I, a voracious reader like Maurine, a school administrator, super athlete and a "saver" and collector. He <u>saves</u> old *Playboys, National Geographic* (about thirty years worth) wine corks, calendars, phonograph records and other goodies. He <u>collects</u> (actively pursues) match boxes, coins, wine, and logo golf balls! He has over 5,000 logo balls from all around the world. Each object of his collections and most savings are meticulously stored, organized, categorized and arranged just so. I think that Lee aspires to "be" Louis Kravetz!

Lee is an excellent athlete and hangs tough in the clutch. I have bowled full or part time with Lee for at least twenty-five years. Lee has twice "struck out" in the tenth frame, of the last game, of the final week, bowling "anchor" (last), after the opposing anchorman had bowled, to win the league championship! I told you that my sister is smart!

One Sunday I was asked to bowl. Afterwards Lee was relaxing, (after the strain of the game) and had a 'quick one' with his lifelong teacher friend Dave Higgins. After a few sips, we were talking baseball. The conversation was lead by yours truly. I informed Higgins that Ruth hit 59 homers in 1921. Higgins flatly denied that fact. I soon pulled out $100 bill out of my pocket and was willing to wager. David is so <u>sure</u> of his knowledge that he quickly accepted the bet. The next week at bowling he could not even remember the discussion! Don't get me wrong, Higgins is a good guy. My family actually named our lovable, koot (derivation of cute) West Highland Terrier after him!

Our dog is named "Higgins". His full name is "Higgins Nolan Ryan Kravetz".

CHAPTER 17

<u>Pitchers That Won The MVP Award</u>

Hopefully baseball fans will at least ask which pitchers have won the Most Valuable Player Award, and were they worthy of this honor. It is obvious that a pitcher may truly have been of the most value to his team in a given year and circumstance, versus a non-pitcher. I do believe that a pitcher should have outstanding credentials due to the fact that he is playing less than the non-pitcher. There is also the possibility that he was the most valuable due to the fact that nobody else had that good of a year! Here, I also give my opinion of who in fact really deserved the award, designated by an (X). It is interesting to also look at pitchers that received the second highest vote total and ask if in fact they deserved to be the league MVP of that season.

I do give some weight to the fact that the player was on the winning team. This weight is in the magnitude of a tie breaker. The reason for this weighted edge is the fact that winning on the field often is a better measurement of value and achieving that common goal, than a retrospective statistical analysis! Winning tends to make up for the shortcoming of statistics.

The MVP award was called the Chalmers Award from 1911-1914. "Prior to the 1910 season, Hugh Chalmers, president and general manager of the Chalmers Motor Company, announced that he would present a Chalmers "30" to the major league player who compiled the highest batting average." This was soon to become a disaster!

The race turned into a two-man fiasco. Detroit's Ty Cobb and Cleveland's Napoleon Lajoie were in a dog fight for the beautiful car and all the pride and bravado that went along with it! "Entering the final day, October 9, Cobb had a .376 mark and chose to sit out his final game. Lajoie played the infamous doubleheader with the St. Louis Browns in which he went 8 for 8, including **seven bunt hits** -- remarkable for a slow-footed slugger -- to apparently edge out Cobb for the title. Browns' manager Jack O'Connor had instructed his rookie third baseman, Red Corriden, to play deep on Lajoie, advice with which Corriden complied. Ban Johnson found a discrepancy in a previous box score of Cobb's and declared Cobb the batting champion! Chalmers awarded both players with a Chalmers "30".

In 1911, Chalmers was to present an auto to the one player in each league who "shall prove himself as the most important and useful player to his club and to the league at large in point of deportment and value of services rendered." There was no stipulation for amount of at-bats for players needed including pitchers, as there was in 1910. All players were eligible. With this, the language and the criteria of an MVP was adopted for future considerations. Between 1915-1921 there were no awards given. That was too bad for the great Bambino. Ruth would have undoubtedly won three more MVP Awards. From 1922-1929 the MVP Award was called the League Award. Since 1931 to present the MVP Award is the Baseball Writer's Association of America Award.

All combined, twenty-three pitchers have won the MVP Award. Seventeen pitchers have placed second in the balloting. Five of those times, pitchers placed second to pitchers.

Pitchers that were named MVP and a synopsis of the statistics are as follows: (**BOLD** denotes league leader).

1913 Walter "The Big Train" Johnson - Washington

W	L	Pct.	GS	CG	IP	H	BB	Ks	ShOut	ERA
36	7	.837	36	**29**	**346**	232	38	**243**	**11**	**1.14**

Comments: No help from a team BA .252. How dare Walter walk 38 men in an amazing 346 innings! Weaver would have pulled him.

Analysis: "Shoeless Joe", Collins, Speaker, Baker, Cobb, Crawford and others had real good years.

(X) Johnson. NO CONTEST!

1924 Walter Johnson, Washington - win.

W	L	Pct.	GS	CG	IP	H	BB	Ks	ShO	ERA
23	7	**.767**	38	20	278	233	77	**158**	6	**2.72**

Babe Ruth NY

AB	R	H	2B	3B	HR	RBI	BB	Ks	AVE	OBP	SA
529	**143**	200	39	7	**46**	121	**142**	81	.378	.513	.739

E. Collins, CHI (2)

AB	R	H	2B	3B	HR	RBI	BB	Ks	AVE	OBP	SA
556	108	194	27	7	6	86	89	16	.349	.441	.455

Comments: No player could be named twice for the League Award! (Ruth '23)

Analysis: Ruth lost his fourth award!

(X) Babe by a landslide, even though Washington did win.

1924 Dazzy Vance - Brooklyn

W	L	Pct.	GS	CG	IP	H	BB	Ks	ShO	ERA
28	6	.824	34	**30**	308	238	77	**262**	3	**2.16**

Rogers Hornsby SL (?)

AB	R	H	2B	3B	HR	RBI	BB	Ks	SB	OBP	AVE	SA
536	**121**	227	**43**	12	14	111	**89**	32	5	**.507**	**.424**	**.696**

Comments: Highest batting average this century!! No pennant winner. You must be kidding!

(X) Hornsby

1931 Lefty Grove A's - win

W	L	Pct.	GS	CG	IP	H	BB	Ks	ShO	ERA
31	4	.886	30	27	289	249	62	175	4	2.05

Gehrig (2)

AB	R	H	2B	3B	HR	RBI	BB	Ks	SB	OBP	AVE	SA
619	163	211	311	5	46	184	117	56	17	.446	.341	.662

Simmons (3) Phi A's - win

AB	R	H	2B	3B	HR	RBI	BB	Ks	SB	OBP	AVE	SA
513	105	200	37	13	22	128	47	45	3		.423	.390	.641

Ruth NY (5)

AB	R	H	2B	3B	HR	RBI	BB	Ks	SB	OBP	AVE	SA
534	149	199	31	3	46	163	128	51	5	.495	.373	.700

Comments: Averill (4) not better than Ruth. Simmons not better than Ruth. Gehrig second highest RBI total in history!

(X) Gehrig for sure, but close!

1933 Hubbell NY - win

W	L	Pct.	GS	CG	IP	H	BB	Ks	ShO	ERA
23	12	.657	33	22	308	256	47	156	10	1.66

Chuck Klein Phi

AB	R	H	2B	3B	HR	RBI	BB	Ks	SB	OBP	AVE	SA
606	101	**223**	**44**	7	**28**	**120**	56	36	15	**.422**	**.368**	**.602**

Comments: Klein wins triple crown! Hubbell gives up 6 HRs!

(X) TIE, or edge to Hubbell

1934 Dizzy Dean SL - win

W	L	Pct.	GS	CG	IP	H	BB	Ks	ShO	ERA
30	7	**.811**	33	24	311	288	75	**195**	7	2.66

AB	R	H	2B	3B	HR	RBI	BB	Ks	SB	OBP	AVE	SA
599	**122**	**217**	32	16	14	90	68	24	8	429	**.362**	.539

(X) Dizzy easily slud in there!

1936 Carl Hubbell NY - win

W	L	Pct.	GS	CG	IP	H	BB	Ks	ShO	ERA
26	6	**.813**	34	25	304	265	57	123	3	2.31

Dizzy Dean SL (2)

W	L	Pct.	GS	CG	IP	H	BB	Ks	ShO	ERA
24	13	.649	34	**28**	315	310	53	195	2	3.17

Comments: Mel Ott good year for champs. Hubbell just 7 HRs, wins last 16 to start his streak of 24!

(X) Hubbell

1939 Bucky Walters Reds - win

W	L	Pct.	GS	CG	IP	H	BB	Ks	ShO	ERA
27	11	.711	36	**31**	**319**	250	109	**137**	2	**2.29**

Johnny Mize SL

AB	R	H	2B	3B	HR	RBI	BB	Ks	OBP	AVE	SA
564	104	197	44	14	**28**	108	92	49	.444	.349	**.626**

Comments: Walters was a former infielder. Reds finished 1st, first time since 1919!

(X) Walters

1942 Mort Cooper SL - win

W	L	Pct.	GS	CG	IP	H	BB	Ks	ShO	ERA
22	7	.759	35	22	297	207	68	152	**10**	**1.78**

Enos Slaughter SL - win (2)

AB	R	H	2B	3B	HR	RBI	BB	Ks	OBP	AVE	SA
591	100	**188**	31	**17**	13	98	88	30	.412	.318	.494

Comments: No Contest
(X) Cooper

1943 Spud Chandler NYY - win

W	L	Pct.	GS	CG	IP	H	BB	Ks	ShO	ERA
20	4	.833	30	**20**	253	197	54	134	**5**	**1.64**

Luke Appling CHI

AB	R	H	2B	3B	HR	RBI	BB	Ks	OBP	AVE	SA
585	63	192	33	2	3	80	90	29	**.419**	**.328**	.407

Comments: Appling, fine year for an infielder, cannot vote against due to lack of power, but definitely Spud.

(X) Chandler

1944 Hal Newhouser DET

W	L	Pct.	GS	CG	IP	H	BB	Ks	ShO	ERA
29	9	.763	34	25	312	264	102	**187**	6	2.22

Dizzy Trout DET

W	L	Pct.	GS	CG	IP	H	BB	Ks	ShO	ERA
27	14	.659	40	**33**	**352**	314	83	144	**7**	**2.12**

Comments: WW II Military absence: (partial) Williams, Appling, Feller, Woodling, Gehringer, Greenberg, Dickey, Gordon, Rizzuto, DiMaggio, Henrich, Collins, Vern Stephens had a good year. Trout a great ERA for 352 innings.

(X) Trout

1945 Hal Newhouser DET - win

W	L	Pct.	GS	CG	IP	H	BB	Ks	ShO	ERA
25	9	**.735**	36	**29**	**313**	239	110	**212**	8	**1.81**

Eddie Mayo DET - win (2)

AB	R	H	2B	3B	HR	RBI	BB	Ks	OBA	AVE	SA
501	71	143	24	3	10	54	47	29	.347	.285	.405

Comments: Mayo a very poor second. Stirnweiss better than Mayo. Many still at war. Newhouser was superb.

(X) Newhouser

1950 Jim Konstanty PHI -win

W	L	Pct.	SV	G	IP	H	BB	Ks	ShO	ERA
16	7	.696	22	74	152	108	50	56	0	2.66

	AB	R	H	HR	RBI	OBP	AVE	SA
Stan Musial SL (2)	555	105	192	28	109	.437	**.346**	**.596**
Eddie Stanky NY (3)	527	115	158	8	51	**.460**	.300	.412
Del Ennis PHI (4)	595	92	185	31	**126**	.372	.311	.551
Duke Snider BRO (9)	620	109	**199**	31	107	.379	.321	.553

Comments: Split Decision. Robin Roberts 20-11, 5 ShO, 309 innings, 3.02.

(X) Del Ennis on the win.

1952
Bobby Shantz A's

W	L	Pct.	GS	CG	IP	H	BB	Ks	ShO	ERA
24	7	**.774**	33	27	279	230	63	152	5	2.48

Allie Reynolds NYY win (2)

W	L	Pct.	GS	CG	IP	H	BB	Ks	ShO	ERA
20	8	.714	35	29	244	194	97	160	**6**	**2.06**

Mickey Mantle NYY - win (3)

AB	R	H	2B	3B	HR	RBI	BB	Ks	OBP	AVE	SA
549	94	171	37	7	23	87	75	111	.394	.311	.530

Comments: Mickey just missed with 87 RBI. Rosen and Doby good years. Shantz lowest on base average against in league 2.72, gold glover.

(X) Shantz.

1956 Don Newcombe BRO - win

W	L	Pct.	GS	CG	IP	H	BB	Ks	ShO	ERA
27	7	**.794**	36	18	268	219	46	139	5	3.06

Sal Maglie BRO - Win (2)

W	L	Pct.	GS	CG	IP	H	BB	Ks	ShO	ERA
13	5	.722	26	9	191	154	52	108	3	2.87

	AB	R	H	HR	RBI	OBP	AVE	SA
Hank Aaron MIL (3)	609	106	**200**	26	92	.369	**.328**	.558
Junior Gilliam BR (5)	594	102	178	6	43	.400	.300	.396
Roy McMillan CIN (6)	479	511	26	3	62	.370	.263	.344
Fr. Robinson CIN (7)	572	**122**	166	38	83	.381	.290	.558
P. Reese BRO (8)	572	85	147	9	46	.324	.257	.344
S. Musial SL (9)	594	87	184	27	**109**	.390	.310	.522
D. Snider BRO (10)	542	112	158	**43**	101	**.402**	.292	**.598**

Comment: Where were the sports writers?

(X) Snider

1963 Sandy Koufax LA - win

Comment: No need to look any farther except for Superman! Aaron (3) had an excellent year, better than Groat (2), McCovey, Mays, Pinson, White and Flood. Koufax 311 innings, 25-5, 306 Ks, 11 ShO, 1.88.

(X) Koufax

1968 "The Year of the Pitcher".

1968 Bob Gibson SL win National

W	L	Pct.	GS	CG	IP	H	BB	Ks	ShO	ERA	OAV	OOB
22	9	.710	34	28	304	198	62	**268**	**13**	**1.12**	**.184**	**.233**

McLain DET - win

W	L	Pct.	GS	CG	IP	H	BB	Ks	ShO	ERA	OAV	OOB
31	6	**.838**	41	**28**	**336**	241	63	280	6	1.96	.200	.233

1968 Denny McLain DET win American

Comments: Rose (N) (2) 210 hits, **.335, .394** OBA had a good year. Freehan (A) (2) did not even deserve second place. Ken Harrelson or Frank Howard did. Besides, McLain "served up" Mickey's 535th on a platter! If any one doesn't still think a pitcher can be a MVP after seeing Koufax, Gibson, and McLain can not be considered a rational baseball fan. The only argument is who was better McLain or Gibson (X)?

(X) Gibson
(X) McLain

1971 Vida Blue OAK - win

W	L	Pct.	GS	CG	IP	H	BB	Ks	ShO	ERA	OAV	OOB
24	8	.750	39	24	312	209	88	301	8	1.82	.189	.252

Sal Bando OAK - win (2)

AB	R	H	2B	3B	HR	RBI	BB	Ks	OBA	AVE	SA
538	75	146	23	1	24	94	86	55	.380	.271	.452

Comments: Frank (3) and Brooks (4) okay. No contest.

(X) Blue

1981 Rollie Fingers MIL -win

W	L	Pct.	SV	IP	H	HR	BB	Ks	ERA
6	3	.667	28	78	55	3	13	61	1.04

Rickey Henderson OAK (2)

AB	R	H	2B	3B	HR	RBI	BB	Ks	SB	OBA	AVE	SA
423	89	135	18	7	6	35	64	68	56	.411	.319	.437

Comments: Mil. could not possibly win without Rollie's brilliant, short-season, performance. Rickey had a good year.

(X) Fingers

1984 Willie Hernandez DET - win

W	L	Pct.	G	SV	IP	H	HR	BB	Ks	ERA
9	3	.750	**80**	32	140	96	6	36	112	1.92

Kent Hrbek MIN (2)

AB	R	H	2B	3B	HR	RBI	BB	Ks	OBA	AVE	SA
559	80	174	31	3	27	107	65	87	.387	.311	.522

Don Mattingly (5)

AB	R	H	2B	3B	HR	RBI	BB	Ks	OBA	AVE	SA
603	91	**207**	**44**	2	23	110	41	33	.386	**.343**	.539

league leader in proficiency, fielding percentage leader
.996, gold glover.

Comments: Hrbek real good year, Mattingly better.
(X) Mattingly

1986 Roger Clemens BOS - win

W	L	Pct.	GS	CG	IP	H	BB	Ks	ShO	ERA
24	4	**.857**	33	10	254	179	67	238	1	**2.48**

Don Mattingly NYY (2)

AB	R	H	2B	3B	HR	RBI	BB	Ks	OBA	AVE	SA
677	117	**238**	**53**	3	31	113	53	35	.399	.352	**.573**

Fielding Pct. .996, gold glove, led league in total bases and game winning hits 15 (Tie) Total Baseball has Don as league leader in proficiency and Batting Runs over average expectation. Even the tall time leader Rose had no more than 230 hits in one given season. (680 AB)

Comments: Clemens delivered 20 over .500. According to **Total Baseball**, Mattingly delivered at least 57 "wins". **IF Clemens deserved the MVP on the division win, THAN SO DID GUIDRY!**

(X) TIE

1992 Dennis Eckersley OAK - win

W	L	Pct.	G	SV	IP	H	HR	BB	Ks	ERA
7	1	.875	69	**51**	80	62	5	11	93	1.91

Kirby Puckett MIN (2)

AB	R	H	2B	3B	HR	RBI	BB	Ks	OBA	AVE	SV
639	104	**210**	38	4	19	110	44	97	.377	.329	.490

Comments: Kirby had a nice year. No contest Eck.

(X) Eckersley

RESULTS 23 Pitchers:

13 Definitely won the MVP

2 Probably won the MVP

2 Tie or too close (one was Trout over Newhouser, pitcher for pitcher)

6 Definitely were not MVP

Pitcher as seconds synopsis:

1911 Frank Schulte vs. Christy Mathewson (X) Rube Marquard (P)

1932 Chuck Klein vs. Lon Warneke (X) Klein

1935 Gabby Hartnett vs. Dizzy Dean (X) Hartnett

1936 Carl Hubbell vs. Dizzy Dean (X) Hubbell (P)

1938 Ernie Lombardi vs. Bill Lee (X) Lee (P)

1944 Hal Newhouser vs. Dizzy Trout (X) Trout (P)

1946 Ted Williams vs. Hal Newhouser (X) Williams

1947 Bob Elliott vs. Ewell Blackwell (X) Elliott

1948 Stan Musial vs. Johnny Sain (X) Tie or Sain (P)

1952 Hank Sauer vs. Robin Roberts (X) Roberts (P)

1952 Bobby Shantz vs. Allie Reynolds (X) Shantz (P)

1956 Don Newcombe vs. Sal Maglie (X) Snider

1958 Jackie Jensen vs. Bob Turley (X) Tie or Turley (P)

1965 Willie Mays vs. Koufax (X) Koufax (P) or Tie

1966 Clemente vs. Koufax (X) Koufax (P)

1969 Willie McCovey vs. Tom Seaver (X) McCovey

1973 Reggie Jackson vs. Jim Palmer (X) Jackson

1978 Jim Rice vs. Ron Guidry (X) Guidry (P)

Interesting enough after a statistical barrage and hundreds of hours of research, the net result is a plus two in favor of pitchers that most definitely won the MVP award!

CHAPTER 18

The Third Largest Ripoff

This is the last of the purely statistical based chapter that will appear in this book. They do serve a purpose for a look at some attitudes of sports writers in their day. It is crystal clear that Teddy boy wasn't their man. He just wasn't the right image! In 1942 and 1947 Williams won the triple crown but was not named the MVP each of those years! *Total Baseball*, once again, gives a wonderful look at this ridiculousness.

Bold print denotes league leader. "PRO + is Production Plus or Adjusted Production (on base percentage plus SA, normalized to league average and adjusted for home-park factor. BR/A is what a league-average batter or team might have contributed."

1942
Joe Gordon NYY 270 votes

AB	R	H	2B	3B	HR	RBI	BB	Ks	OBA	AVE	SA	PRO+	BR/A
538	88	173	29	4	18	103	79	95	.409	.322	.491	119	14

Ted Williams BOS 249 votes

AB	R	H	2B	3B	HR	RBI	BB	Ks	OBA	AVE	SA	PRO+	BR/A
522	**141**	186	34	5	**36**	**137**	**145**	51	**.499**	**.356**	**.648**	**214**	**8**

1947

Joe DiMaggio NYY 202 votes

AB	R	H	2B	3B	HR	RBI	BB	Ks	OBA	AVE	SA	PRO+	BR/A
534	97	168	31	10	20	97	64	32	.391	.315	.522	154	38
528	**125**	181	40	9	**32**	114	162	47	**.499**	**.343**	**.634**	199	**79**

Ted Williams BOS 201 votes! ARE YOU KIDDING?

Well Ted, if it is any consolation the GREAT HONUS WAGNER, who could play any position except pitcher, better than anyone else, should have been the MVP in 1900, 1901, 1902, 1903, 1907, 1909, 1912.

But of course the Babe was the greatest of all time. He won the MVP in 1923. Because of no awards given or funky rules, that was Ruth's only award! His record should look like this: Sure wins 1918, 1920, 1921, 1923, 1924, 1926, 1927, 1928, 1930, 1931. That is TEN! and probably in 1929 and 1932!

CHAPTER 19

<u>The Captain Goes out on Top</u>

Last night, on that famous night of October 8,. the Yankees went down to defeat as the first "wild card" series. This day was not as fortunate as thirty-nine years previous. Pitching and fundamentals are still the name of the game. For all the million-dollar sluggers there are, it came down to inability of Randy Velarde to bunt and the uncanny ability of Joey Cora to beat Donzie, with a perfect bunt.

David Cone was valiant in his attempt to finish off the Mariners in their funky park. Black Jack McDowell also poured his heart and soul out in his valiant effort with just two days rest. It's obvious that McDowell is no James Augustus Hunter , who won the World Series by saving a final game, for the great Rollie Fingers! Catfish is also the last Yankee pitcher to win a final game, in a year when the Yankees took it all. (1978) Not by coincidence, Captain Munson was the catcher. It is also obvious that John Wetteland is no Rolland Fingers and Randy Johnson is not the equal of Sandy Koufax.

In the end it was the hardness of the carpet that ruled. What has this game come to? On normal grass Pat Kelly would have speared Griffey's extra inning single, Edgar's ball would not have rolled to the wall and the Captain Don definitely would have cleared the bases with his clutch double, instead of a ground rule double, which drove in just two. In the final analysis it was a Joey Cora bunt that was the key *blow!*

If there is a golden lining, it is that Donzie won the last games he played, at the "House That Ruth Built." The Captain was truly worthy of his title. He had an amazingly productive September, when the Yankees were in a must situation for nearly six weeks. The only rest that they had was when they went into Boston, and easily took three in a row, to keep their dream of a "wild card" berth alive. This time was really only a "Mini Boston Massacre"!

"Donnie Baseball" went out with *class*. He truly ex-emplified the Yankee Pride, even as Steinbrenner tried to put him out to the pasture. He handled all discussions with dignity. He, although not perfect, is still truly the "gold glover" of the league, and is going for number 10 in 1995! Mattingly also displayed some power, even with a deteriorated back condition. Captain Don always had the knack of hitting in the clutch as proven in the "Card Race", the Division Series and his entire

173

career. There is **no** doubt that he was a special cut above, for his career, and definitely Hall of Famer. Thanks Donzie. You are a true Yankee.

CHAPTER 20

FFAB

I was born in February of 1949. The fact of the matter is that I was also premature by two months. It wasn't until that I began to write this book that it became evident to me that the early arrival was meant to be. I had to be out on time for opening day and the beginning of the greatest Yankee dynasty! Although I still want to "be" Mickey Mantle, I am finally starting to realize that time is beginning to slip away! I would now need to find the fountain of youth. Now I want to "be" Marvin Miller, but to represent the fan's interest!

About a year ago, I was called into the home office of my employer. I am employed by Merck & Co Inc, arguably the best pharmaceutical company in the world. I have been blessed with meeting so many class people who do so much good for mankind.

During a break, I was chatting with my co-worker Felicia Forma. She is quite intelligent, extremely creative and likes to talk about ideas. I mentioned that the fans need a vehicle to fight back against the owners and players. What voice do the lowly fans have against the powerful and intimidating "argument between millionaires and billionaires" as author David Halberstam has so properly stated? Over lunch Felicia, Denise Sawyer and I coined the organization of Fans For Affordable Baseball. The FFAB.

The mission of the FFAB is to be the "voice of the fans" and to ensure that the Game survives! The membership fee to join the FFAB would be a mere $5.00 or any larger donation that one could afford to send in to the cause. A log of all members would be carefully kept, because numbers of enrollees would create power for the fans to fight back during these ridiculous and greedy strikes. Nearly all moneys would be appropriated for the cause, with just a nominal expenses allocated to send out membership cards. The FFAB would then target specific dates and games where participation, which means watching and attending games, would be highly discouraged. National newspaper ads such as *USA Today* would carry our message. We would enhance our effectiveness by zeroing in on key markets, cities, weekends around holidays, rivalries and pennant races.

The FFAB executive director would ultimately have the power to negotiate specific points with the millionaires and billionaires. First, increases in ticket prices, concession stands and parking would have to be tied to the Consumer Price Index. Ultimately the FFAB will demand a percentage of the television revenue, which will go back into strengthening the organization.

The voice of the fan MUST be heard in order to save the great American pastime. Baseball should realize that this will evolve anyway so why not involve the fans today?

Please note: the following predictions are for true baseball romanticists only!! If you do not qualify please skip to the next chapter!

- This book will sell enough copies to enable the author to donate enough money to buy Pittsford Little League the baseball complex that is long overdue. Now, every kid will be able to play ball if so desired. One teacher in the Pittsford School District, Mrs. Blanchard, will start a brand new spelling list with her young pupils. The first three words will read: Practice, Makes, Perfect.

- Uncle George will get wind of this book and send its author four lifetime lower boxes next to the Yankee dugout. The only stipulation will be that the author and his family or friends must attend at least eighty games a year, or else there will be an "unequivocal revocation of the seats." George is known for driving hard bargains!

- A new young player named Thurman will win the Rookie of the Year award. Before signing a new contract, he will demand that *he* will have to call every pitch or else will quit. Management will be appalled at losing their best stall tactic to sell "baseball time" to the public. Thurman will then catch every game of the next

177

entire season but <u>never once</u> look over to the dugout. The Yankees win the World Series and this "despicable display of attitude and understanding of the game" will become a major insult to the "brain trust" in the dugout. The owner, who wants to be Commissioner, will tell them all to "shut up"!

- Baseball will get a commissioner *some time* by the 21st Century. The best man is definitely Bill White.

- The Orthopedic Surgeons of the country will be the busiest physicians in the world. With their extraordinary stress levels and discretionary funds in their pockets, it will soon be realized that every ORS has season box seats, in a major league city. The doctors will soon organize, and discuss their common problem of getting to the baseball games on time. Soon thereafter, they will lobby the Surgeon General Pedro Seitz who wants to "be" Commissioner, and he then mandates that Astroturf is strictly prohibited. Thank God!

- The FFAB takes off in fine fashion and baseball survives. The constituents demand that the executive director lives in one of those magnificent captain's houses, overlooking the water, on Coronado beach. Naturally this demand must be complied with "for the good of the game."

- Bill Gates buys every team in the USA and Canada including their farm systems. He announces that this reorganization plan will have two leagues, one will be the APBA National and the other will be the APBA American. There will be eight teams in each league, 154 games, and a World Series. All games will be played in open air stadiums, on natural green grass that has been freshly double cut in a criss-cross pattern, with wooden bats and enforcing the pine tar rule. One-half of all games including the World Series, must be played during the day in sunlight. He will allow pepper games anywhere in the ball park, but not with "raised seamers".

Gates purchases all the JUGS guns in the world and renames them to be politically correct. The only time that the letters DH are allowed in the ball park is on hats dedicated to the memory of the late Jerry Garcia. All announcers must be "Hall of Famers" or have written a book about baseball proving their profound insight. All children born in the western hemisphere are soon thereafter sent a transistor radio with a small ear piece included. The radios will have MSFT engraved on each one. All MSFT computer programs will also drop their asterisk (*) capabilities.

The executive director of the FFAB also becomes the chairperson of the committee to elect future "Hall of Famers". Roger, Thurman and Pete finally gain admission.

This new arrangement gains total acceptance and lives on as the "new and improved" MSFT American pastime.

CHAPTER 21

<u>2001 The Renewed Rivalry</u>

The year was 1984. Rose collected hit number 4,000 playing for Montreal. Doc Gooden was smoking the National League as the Rookie of the Year, Sparky had the Tigers off to a great start which also easily held up to the end and Bill Buckner was already playing for Boston.

The Yankees showed some life. Willie Randolph was still real dependable. Steve Kemp, Butch Wynegar, and Don Baylor were productive and at times exciting. Ken Griffey Sr. was chipping in and so was part-timer Lou Piniella (.302).

David Mark Winfield and Donald Arthur Mattingly ended up with 400 hits between them. The October showdown for the Yankees was for the American League batting title. Don and Dave came down to the last day.

It was great that it had come down to two Yankees. If people were rooting for Don because he was white and Dave black, then Abraham Lincoln, Jackie Robinson, Martin Luther King and the United States and all of mankind failed. If people were rooting for "Donnie Baseball" because he was their favorite Yankee, then that was fine and understandable. It was definitely okay and understandable to root for Mickey instead of Roger in 1960 and 1961.

In the year 2001 both players will become eligible for the Hall of Fame. Let me state up front that there is no question that David Winfield belongs in the Hall of Fame for his career accomplishments. He was a remarkable athlete who amassed over 3,100 hits along with 465 Home Runs and was an exceptional fielder. He performed weakly in his first World Series (Mr. May) but redeemed himself in the 1992 World Series by knocking in the go-ahead run for Toronto in the clutch (game six). In All-Star competition he hit .361 and won seven gold gloves in his career. He also made the best catch that I have ever seen, leaping into the left-center field stands at Yankee Stadium.

Don Mattingly and Dave Winfield had parallel careers in the sense that they both warmed up, had their prime streaks, injured their backs and finished out their careers.

I truly believe that Mattingly was better in his streak than was Winfield. This has nothing to do with race, religion or any other prejudices. David played longer (22 years to 14 years) and amassed outstanding numbers.

Don's streak of excellence lasted six years, from 1984-1989. David's streak of excellence lasted seven years,

1982-1988.

Don M

	AB	H	2B	Hrs	RBI	BA	SLG	League Leading Stats
	3731	1222	257	160	684			12
6 yr Ave.	622	204	43	27	114	.328	.529	

Dave

	AB	H	2B	Hrs	RBI	BA	SLG	League Leading Stats
	4036	1173	208	190	744			1
7 yr Ave.	577	168	30	27	106	.291	.501	

Don has won more gold gloves (9-7) and hit over .400 in post season play.

Dave hit longer line drives and was a better home run hitter.

The new millennium should see both great Yankees enter the Hall of Fame together.

CHAPTER 22

<u>2002 - The Yankees are a Sure Thing!</u>

When we grew up, Mickey and the Yankees were a "sure thing". Times have radically changed with strikes and outlandish contracts and the like, but the American pastime will live on! There is too much order and tradition in the world of baseball to think otherwise.

Why are people so hung up about numbers? What is the difference between the lifetime average of .298 and .300, did this make Mickey any worse? Is the 50th All-star game more important than the 51st? Is it because we are so rushed and need easy pithy formulas to express ourselves, or is it the influence of marketing and Madison Ave.! It seems that it also human nature to make things neat and tidy. Maybe that is why the fifties were a great time to grow up. Or was it the fact that we were awe struck with Babe and Lou and always compared each team with the '27 Yankees? Or was it meant to be that the Yankees won in '27, '52, and '77 (Reggie). Each was obviously a neat and tidy, twenty five years apart.

In 1927 the greatest Yankees played in the World Series and Babe again out shined poor Lou. Mark Koenig was the real hero, along with solid pitching and the rest of the mighty Yankees lineup. The Yankees swept the Pirates 4-0 to end a spectacular season.

In 1952 the Yankees with a young Mickey knocked off "dem Bums" as usual. Mickey hit his first of eighteen World Series homeruns, which is still a record. He followed that homer up with a grand slam and led the Yankees to their fourth consecutive World Championship with 10 hits. The great Reynolds and Raschi combination won two games each. Each had a super ERA of well under 2.0! (1.77, 1.59).

In 1977 the Yankees, as usual beat the Dodgers, as Reggie's heroics caught up with his mouth! He earned his Yankee pinstripes with a flare and enshrined himself wearing the NY hat. Even Munson was impressed with his performance!

In 2002 or 2003, because of the latest strike, the Yankees **will** win the World Series. It is certain that the Captain will be sitting behind the plate. His father's memory will drive him pragmatically. He will hit in every game, drive in key runs, and throw out runners in critical situations. Young Munson will do all it takes to make his team World Champions.

CHAPTER 23

2018

"THE RED SOX WIN THE WORLD SERIES. THE RED SOX WIN THE WORLD SERIES. THE RED SOX WIN THE WORLD SERIES. THE RED SOX WIN THE WORLD SERIES. I DON'T BELIEVE IT! I DON'T BELIEVE IT! I DON'T BELIEVE!!!!

... Yes sports fans of the world you **have** heard me **right! THE BOSTON RED SOX ARE THE WORLD CHAMPIONS OF 2018!!!!**"

I can clearly hear Russ Hodges screaming in the microphone, with amazement!

Finally the "curse of the Bambino" has been broken. The last Series win was in the year 1918 with the Babe pitching for the home team Red Sox. Maybe God is being good to Billy Buckner in the ninth inning. Understand that it really wasn't Buckner's fault! He was just the mortal messenger. That ground ball hit by Mookie Wilson, and all the other generations of heartbreaks including Pesky getting surprised by Enos Slaughter in 1946, DiMaggio's phenomenal comebacks, Johnny Lindell's tie-breaking homer in the second last game and Raschi's complete game to clinch in 1949, and **the** Bucky Dent home run off Mike Torres in 1978 to complete blowing a 14 game lead over the Yankees, are clearly the fault of Harry Frazee.

It was Frazee that traded the young George Herman Ruth, in January of 1920, to the Yankees because he needed money to underwrite his theater productions. The price was $100,000, a $300,000 loan, and five generations of misery for the Red Sox fans! A large asterisk should be put into "the book, and it should read **** **LARGEST ERROR IN BASEBALL HISTORY, TRADED BABE RUTH!**

For the record, Buckner was a damn good hitter with the Dodgers and Cubbies. He led the league in average with .324 in 1980 and doubles twice (1981, 1983). He was an excellent clutch hitter and was not noted for a particularly weak glove, as some might think.

Ralph Branca was a very good pitcher in his career before October of 1951. He had previously won 21 games in 1947! He also had seasons of winning 14, 13, and 13 games in that 1951 season. Maybe the real problem was that he wore number 13 on his uniform, but also the fact that Thomson had recently "seen the rotation" and hit one off Branca just two days earlier. Fred "Bonehead" Merkle (.273 lifetime batting average, 271 stolen bases) and Mickey Owens (.255 lifetime average for a catcher) were not bad ball players, although Merkle was a rookie, nor were they bad men! We just have demanding fans. That is why the great American pastime will live on forever and ever.

PS: Ending this book on this note may upset my friends but this exemplifies the beauty of our great game. Even after one hundred years, you may see something that is as incomprehensible as Boston winning a World Series! Will miracles never cease? Besides my friends Tim Weckworth and Jon Curran will finally be happy. We all know that life is much too short, so be sure to play *a lot* of innings!

After writing this article, I came across a very nice baseball blooper book written by Dan Gutman. Obviously we were on the same wave length as the curse of the Bambino and Harry Frazee! *(Baseball's Biggest Bloopers,* Penguin USA).

Bibliography

Adelson, Bruce, Beaton, Rod Koenig, Rod, Winston, Lisa. *The Minor League Baseball Baseball Book.* New York: Macmillan, USA, 1995.

Brown, Gene, ed. *The New York Times Scrapbook Encyclopedia of Sports History.* New York. Arno Press.

Carter, Craig, ed. *The Sporting News Complete Baseball Record Book.* St. Louis, MO.: The Sporting News Publishing Co., 1994.

Creamer,. Robert W. *Babe.* New York: Penguin Books, 1983.

Creamer, Robert W., *Stengel: His Life and Times.* New York: Fireside Books, 1989.

Davids, L. Robert, ed. *Insider Baseball: The Finer Points of the Game.* New York: Charles Scribner's Sons, 1983.

Devaney, John, Goldblatt, Burt. *The World Series: A Complete Pictorial History.* Chicago: R. and McNally & Company.

Einstein, Charles, ed. *The Fireside Book of Baseball.* New York: Simon and Schuster, 1956.

Gallagher, Mark. *The Yankee Encyclopedia.* New York: Leisure Press, 1982.

Gutman, Dan. *Baseball's Biggest Bloopers; The Games That Got Away.* New York: Viking Penguin Books, 1993.

Halberstam, David. *October 1964.* New York: Villard Books, 1994.

Heylar, John. *Lords of the Realm: The Real History of Baseball.* New York: Villard Books, 1994.

Honig, Donald. *Baseball America: The Heroes of the*

Game and the Times of Their Glory. New York: Macmillan Publishing Co., 1985.

Koppett, Leonard. *The New Thinking Fan's Guide to Baseball.* New York: Simon and Schuster, 1991.

Miller, Marvin. *A Whole Different Ball Game: The Sport and Business of Baseball.* New York: Birch Lane Press, 1991.

Murray, Tom, ed. *Sport Magazine's All-Time Stars.* New York: The New American Library, Inc. 1977.

Neft, David S, Cohen, Richard M. *The Sports Encyclopedia: Baseball; 1995 Edition.* New York: St,. Martin's Press, 1995.

Reichler, Joseph L., ed. *The Baseball Encyclopedia: The Complete And Official Record of Major League Baseball.* New York: Macmillan Publishing Company, 1985.

Reidenbaugh, Lowell. *The Sporting News: The First Hundred Years.* St. Louis, Missouri: The Sporting News, 1985.

Schlossberg, Dan. *The Baseball Catalogue.* Middle Village, New York: Jonathan David Publishers, Inc. 1980.

Thorn, John, ed. Palmer, Pete, ed. Gershman, Michael, ed., Pietrusza, David, managing ed. *Total Baseball IV: The Official Encyclopedia of Major League Baseball.* New York: Viking, Penguin Books, 1995.

Did you want to be Mickey Mantle or any other superstar growing up, then this book is for you. Take a trip down memory lane and enjoy the happy moments of growing up in the fifties and sixties. Life was less structured and demanding. Mickey, baseball and the Yankees are what you lived for!

ORDER FORM

* Fax orders: (716) 381-8123
   On-line orders: GK Creations
   Book order @ gkcreations.com
   Postal orders: Robert Kravetz
                                 5 Whitecliff Dr.
                                 Pittsford, N.Y. 14534

Please send the following books:

_____

_____

_____

_____

  Inquire about discounts on ten or more books
Sales tax:
  Please add 8 percent for books shipped to N.Y.S. addresses
Shipping: Book rate: 1.75 for the first book and 50 cents each additional book.

PLEASE ENCLOSE CHECK
FOLLOWING PLACEMENT OF ORDERS

Epilogue

A French philosopher once said that to know America well, one must first study the game of baseball.

Baseball is the warp and woof of the American fabric. You are working with human clay. It is the stuff that heroes are made of.

So we give thanks to Abner Doubleday and his followers, and we give thanks also to Babe Ruth and Lou Gehrig, to Jackie Robinson and Cal Ripken and to my very special hero, Mickey Mantle, who enhanced my youth with thrills and excitement.

And another round of thanks to the late great Morrie Silver, whose vision and determination saved baseball in Rochester in the 1950s. And to his courageous and lovely wife, Anna Silver, who nurtured and strengthened the tradition and their astute and talented daughter, Naomi, who is chief operating officer of Rochester Community Baseball Inc. And good luck to everybody as the scene shifts from storied Silver Stadium to the new, state-of-the-art Frontier Field, hard by the home of Eastman Kodak Co. in a revitalized section of downtown Rochester. We are looking forward to all the Kodak moments the future holds.